READER

Robyn Christensen

Australia & New Zealand A to Z

Cornelsen
& OXFORD

Die Serie – **Reader** – wurde geplant von der Verlagsredaktion
und entwickelt mit den Verfasserinnen und Verfassern.

Australia A to Z

Verfasserin Robyn Christensen

Verlagsredaktion Dr. Blanca-Maria Rudhart

Layout/Herstellung Axel Jens Penner

Umschlag Axel Jens Penner

1. Auflage
5. 4. 3. | Die letzten Ziffern bezeichnen
1998 97 | Zahl und Jahr des Druckes.

Alle Drucke dieser Auflage können, weil untereinander unverändert,
im Unterricht nebeneinander verwendet werden.

Bestellnummer **31888**

Reproduktionen Schütte & Behling, Berlin

Gesamtherstellung Saladruck, Berlin

Vertrieb Cornelsen Verlag, Berlin

ISBN 3 – 8109 – 3188 – 8

Gedruckt auf Recyclingpapier, hergestellt aus 100% Altpapier.

Contents

Introduction

If a tunnel were dug through the centre of the earth from Western Europe, the opening on the other side would come out near Australia and New Zealand (swimming or boating equipment would be necessary). Anyone wishing to travel from Western Europe cannot choose a destination that is more distant. This distance played an important role in the European settlement and development of both these countries in the southern hemisphere. Distance, in all of Australia, is still a major factor influencing many aspects of life there today. Space and distance are the two aspects which surprise and amaze many visitors today. When visiting New Zealand, many people are also surprised at the length from north to south. Often visitors find themselves down towards the tip of the South Island, a long way from their departure point in the North Island. This may mean a long, hurried trip has to be made to catch a plane on time. Distances in New Zealand seem often longer than in Europe because the roads follow the coastline or valleys. The scenery is beautiful. Freeways comparable to the motorway system in Europe are almost non-existent in both countries, and there are many unsealed roads.

Australia and New Zealand A to Z is a collection of articles for anyone interested in finding out something about the two countries, regardless of whether a visit is planned or not. The book is for any reader with an upper intermediate level of English. It can also be used as an introduction for more advanced readers. The articles can be read in any order. However, at the end of each one there is a list of others which are connected in some way and could be read together. The vocabulary list at the back explains both special terms from the countries and the more difficult general vocabulary. Often the meaning of a word can be discovered by reading the text a little further, and the vocabulary list can then be used to check the exact meaning.

Robyn Christensen

Animals

Australia has been cut off from other continents by the ocean for about fifty million years. The early primitive mammals or warm-blooded animals, especially the marsupials, survived and evolved in isolation, free from competition from the more advanced mammals. There are about 230 species of mammals in Australia. Almost half of these are marsupials, animals with an external pouch. The young marsupials are tiny when born and make their way from the womb to the pouch by themselves. They are too small for the mother to help them. Often she will make a path for them across her fur by licking it. Once in the pouch, the young find the mother's milk and stay there until they have fully developed. The young animal will then begin to leave the pouch for short periods. As it develops, it stays outside for longer, returning only to drink the milk or for safety. The other mammals in Australia are monotremes, egg-laying mammals, and the common placental mammals such as dingoes, the wild dogs, possums and mice.

Wombats are marsupials which look a little like a small bear. They grow to just over a metre, weigh about 40 kilograms and have black, brown or grey fur with a pouch opening backwards. Their tails are very small, their legs short and the head is wide with small ears. They are very sociable creatures, living in burrows usually connected with tunnels to the rest of the colony. By instinct they go through things rather than around and are often considered stupid and destructive. If an enemy follows it down the burrow, the wombat crushes it against the roof using the bony plate in its rump, the area around the tail. Apart from this, they are not aggressive. Some live on the plains, others in the forest. They are vegetarians and most active at dawn and dusk.

Koalas have very sharp claws on their toes making movement and living in trees possible. As marsupials, the mothers carry their young while they are small in their pouch, and later on their backs. Mature females of at least three years normally have one young each year. There are only a few of the native eucalyptus or gum trees that the koalas can eat. They live on the leaves of the manna, messmate, swamp, peppermint and mahogany gum trees. Koalas only come down to the ground to move to another tree, and seldom drink water. They feed at, night, sometimes in small groups, grunting occasionally like a pig. During the day they normally rest in a fork of a tree, and often look very sleepy. There is said to be something in the gum leaves that makes them "high", as if they had taken drugs.

The **platypus** is one of the two types of monotremes that are alive today. Its body is covered with dark brown, dense, water-resistant fur and its webbed feet help it swim. When looking for food, the platypus dives to the bottom of the creek or river pools. It finds shrimps and other delicacies with its electronically sensitive bill. Scientific experiments have shown that its bill is a miniature radar system, sensing the size and location of living things by the electronic impulses it sends out. Its eyes are closed at all times under water and food is temporarily stored in its cheeks. It digs tunnels above the water line within the river banks for its home. Spring is the mating time and 1-3 eggs are laid within two weeks. In about another ten days the eggs hatch.

see also Bunyips; Dingoes; Quokkas

Artesian Water

Artesian water is water below the surface that fell as rain a large distance away. It normally takes a long time to reach the artesian basin at its lowest point as it flows within the earth. In Australia the artesian water is very important for the large cattle and sheep stations in the inland. The water is alkaline and not suitable for people to drink. The quality of the water is also too low to use for irrigation projects as the mineral content is too high. However, cattle and sheep can drink it and therefore this water has made it possible to open up large areas of arid land in inland Australia for grazing.

The Great Artesian Basin is approximately 1.7 million square kilometres, the largest of five in Australia. The water falls in Queensland as rain on the western side of the Great Dividing Range which runs the whole length of the east coast. The rain runoff seeps into the earth and into a wide band of porous or non-solid rock. This band of rock full of water then drops down into the earth below the surface. Further west it flattens out but continues to drop a little deeper as it goes. This drop is enough to make the water in the rock flow slowly west. The rock band continues across the continent to below the Great Western Plateau. Below this porous rock layer is one of solid rock. The solid rock stops the water from flowing deeper and being lost in the depths of the earth. Both these would not be enough for artesian water to form, but just west of the Great Dividing Range another layer of impermeable or solid rock begins. This layer covers the surface of most of the Great Western Plateau and

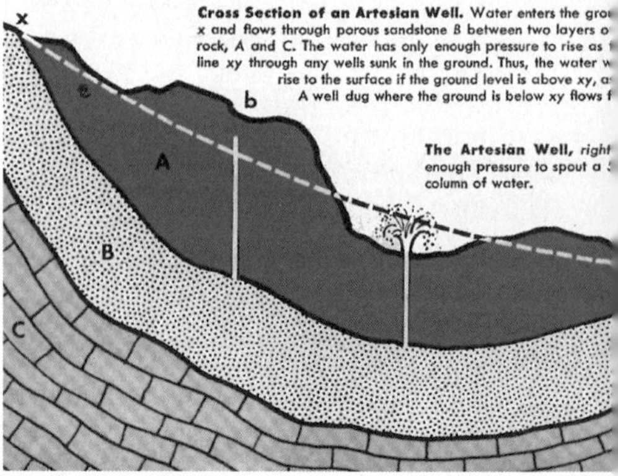

Cross Section of an Artesian Well. Water enters the gro
x and flows through porous sandstone *B* between two layers o
rock, *A* and C. The water has only enough pressure to rise as
line *xy* through any wells sunk in the ground. Thus, the water w
rise to the surface if the ground level is above *xy*, a
A well dug where the ground is below *xy* flows f

The Artesian Well, *right*
enough pressure to spout a
column of water.

normally stops the water from reaching the surface and evaporating with the heat. The artesian water is trapped between two layers of rock. This geological structure was discovered in the dry Australian outback when some natural artesian springs were found. Water is always precious in dry areas and investigations were made. The artesian water is under pressure and in some places comes to the surface in the form of mineral springs which are often warm. In many areas, the pressure is not strong enough to bring the water to the surface. There, where a bore is dug mechanical, pumps or windmills are necessary. A common sight in the outback is windmills, alone or in groups. These are often the only landmark in an area with mainly low plants and few, if any, trees.
When artesian water is found, the bores are dug at regular intervals. These intervals are the distance cattle and sheep can travel without water. Native birds and animals also take advantage of these water supplies. It is quite common to see kangaroos feeding around a bore and flocks of green, yellow or blue budgerigars or brightly coloured parrots flying or drinking.

see also Australia - Areas and Regions; Bushfires

Australia – Areas and Regions

Australia is the fifth and smallest continent. It covers approximately 7,700,000 square kilometres, the mainland is almost 4,000 kilometres from west to east and over 3,000 kilometres from north to south. Most of the land is very flat. The very old **Western Plateau** is generally only 300 metres above sea-level and is mostly desert or semi-desert. In general Australia's climate has a mild drought or dry period every five years and a bad one every ten. One example is **Central Australia** which went without rain for seven years in the 1970s. Therefore, although the soil may be fertile in the inland, little or no water makes it almost impossible for people to live there and use the land. Much of the water that has managed to reach these dry areas over hundreds of years and run into the lake system has brought salt to the surface. The heat evaporates the water. As the lakes dry out the water just below the surface rises because of the heat and also evaporates on the surface bringing up salts from the soils. The Western Plateau contains many salt lakes. Lake Eyre, the largest, covers an area of over 9,000 square kilometres and as the lowest is 16 metres below sea-level. It is the drainage basin of the inland river system that confused the early settlers who thought the area would be well supplied with fresh water. Due to these conditions there are only the two large settlements of Darwin in the north and Alice Springs in the Centre.

The Tropics are in the north and have wet and dry seasons controlled by the monsoons, wet seasonal rains blowing south from the equator. The wet season normally starts in November and continues to April. Rainfalls are heavy and continual, often washing out roads and making travel across the country impossible. Planes can only land on sealed or concrete airfields and not on any flat area of cleared ground. Thick, tall tropical rain forest still covers large areas of the north-east. Only 3% of the population live in the north, again because of the climate.

The Great Dividing Range runs along the east coast from north to south. Its name describes what it does – to divide the continent into two main areas. The mountain range, although not very high, forces the moister air coming from the ocean to the east to rise. The air cools and the water in it falls as rain. The mountains themselves and the eastern coastal regions have much more rain.
West of the Great Dividing Range the yearly rainfall drops until the desert areas are reached. About one third of the continent receives under 25 cm of rain each year and another third between 25 and 50 cm a year.
Australia is the driest continent on earth. The Great Dividing Range has Australia's highest mountain, Mount Kosciusko, in the "Australian Alps". The Australian Alps are relatively low by world standards and were covered with glaciers. They are steep, rugged and covered with native eucalyptus forest.
Most of the population live in the east and south-east coastal areas, especially around the cities of Melbourne, Sydney, Adelaide and Brisbane. Other areas where more people live are **Tasmania** which is cut off from the mainland by Bass Strait. It has a much milder climate with snow each winter and about 3% of the population live there. Around 17% of the Australian population live on the south-west coast around Perth, where the climate is warm, but pleasant and rainfall is enough to support farms and a large city.

see also Artesian Water

Australia and Europe

When a map of Australia is put on one of a similar scale of Europe the size of Australia is easier to understand. Space and openness are two features that are special and important in Australia, especially in relationship to the relatively small population of 18,289,000 (June '96).

Starting at the most south-east point of Australia and moving anti-clockwise, Tasmania crosses the Mediterranean Sea and extends into Egypt, while Sydney to the north lies in central Turkey. The most north-east point of Australia, Cape York, is a third of the way along the border between Finland and Russia. The north coast of Australia then crosses central Sweden and Norway, and goes down to the south-west to include Scotland and touches the coast of Ireland. The fifth continent's coast moves further west and then south through Portugal and includes most of Spain. Australia's long south coast starts with its most western part running through the Mediterranean Sea south of Spain and runs east enclosing most of Italy and Greece.

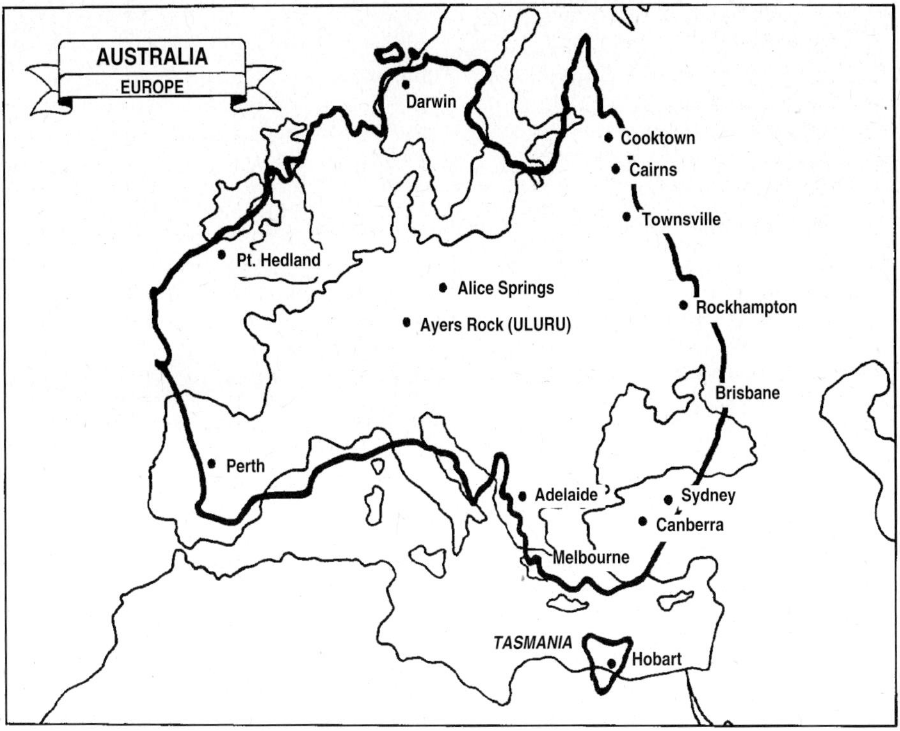

see also Artesian Water; Australian Capital Territory; Great Barrier Reef; Journeys Inland; National Parks; New South Wales; Northern Territory; Outback Life; Queensland; Rain-Making; Settlement of Australia; South Australia; Tasmania; Todd River; Uluru and the Red Centre; Victoria; West Australia; Zeehan

Australian Capital Territory

The Australian Capital Territory or A. C. T. is an area of over 150 square kilometres. The area is in the Australian Alps and some parts normally have snow in winter. Winter days are often sunny, clear and cold and in summer temperatures may reach the high 30° or 40° centigrade although the nights can be cold.
Canberra is the national capital and is in the A. C. T.
Canberra lies on the plains of the Molongo Valley, about 600 metres above sea-level. The area around the city is used mainly for sheep grazing and it varies from open plains to hills with low snow gums and scrub. The Molongo River runs through the city. Lake Burley Griffin and a chain of lakes through the city were made along the river. The city and suburbs were designed by Walter Burley Griffin and have many trees and open spaces as well as circular streets and avenues with trees. Over two million native and non-native trees have been planted in Canberra. Sometimes it is called the "garden city". The architect's aim was to design streets and buildings that fitted into the natural landscape.
The population was 1,150 in 1921 and 307,500 in 1996. Even today, however, Canberra is still more the official capital only, and Melbourne and Sydney are really more important.

see also New South Wales; Politics; Victoria

Beaches

Most Australians live on or near the coast, and as the climate is warm and hot in summer, swimming, surfing, fishing, diving and being on the beach is an integral part of life.
The method of swimming called the crawl or freestyle was developed in Australia early this century.
The long summer holidays normally mean beach and swimming and many families go for a traditional swim or surf on Christmas Day. With over 36,000 kilometres of coastline and an average of two people per square kilometre, beaches, not crowded or empty, are easy to find. Although some of the coast is rugged and only cliffs, long beaches of yellow and white sand are in all states with calm water or surf. All of the popular surf beaches have life-saving clubs. Members, all voluntary, watch the ocean for swimmers in distress who need to be saved and also clear the water in case of sharks. Younger members are taught surf swimming techniques, life-saving techniques, resuscitation and first aid. Later they learn about the "rubber duckie", the inflatable boats with outboard motors used to save swimmers having problems in heavy surf. There are competitions between clubs from a local to a national level.
The feelings of an Australian "surfie":
When yer drivin' hard 'n' fast down the wall, with a soup curlin' behind yer, or doin' this bagside turn on a big one about ter tube, it's jus' this feeling. Yer know . . . , that is, "When you are driving hard and fast down the wall (of the wave), with the white top of the wave curling behind you, or doing this backside turn on a big one about to tube (the top of the wave rolls over to make a tube which the surfer can ride through), it's just this feeling. You know . . ."

see also Australia – Areas and Regions; New Zealand – Areas and Regions; South Australia; Yachting and Sailing

Boomerangs

A boomerang is a hunting tool made by the Kooris, the first people of Australia. It is a flat, curved piece of wood that everyone has heard of because when it is thrown properly it returns to the thrower. The Kooris developed the boomerang from the throwing stick which was used to knock out and kill animals when hunting. There are many boomerangs used for different jobs. All Koori tribes did not have all types, in fact, some did not have any at all. The heavier, non-returning boomerang was used for hunting. Traditionally it was made from a curved branch of the native mulga tree. This is a small tree with a twisted trunk, narrow leaves and yellow flowers that grows in the dry inland regions. The top side of the boomerang is rounded and the lower side is flat, having one wing or arm much longer than the other. The largest boomerangs are up to two metres in length and were also used as a general tool around the camp. Areas were flattened and cleared of grass with longer boomerangs, the fire was often looked after and pushed together with a boomerang and, occasionally, cooked animals were cut up using the sharp end of a boomerang.

The well-known returning boomerang is light and thin and was only used by a limited number of tribes. It flies because of highly complicated aerodynamic principles. These boomerangs were used mainly for sport. Hunting was limited to killing birds and hitting animals from a distance to send them towards traps. The Boomerang Association of Australia holds annual championships in boomerang throwing.

see also Kooris; Boomerang Construction

Boomerang Construction

A boomerang has one side that is flat, the back, and the other, the front, is rounded and shaped.

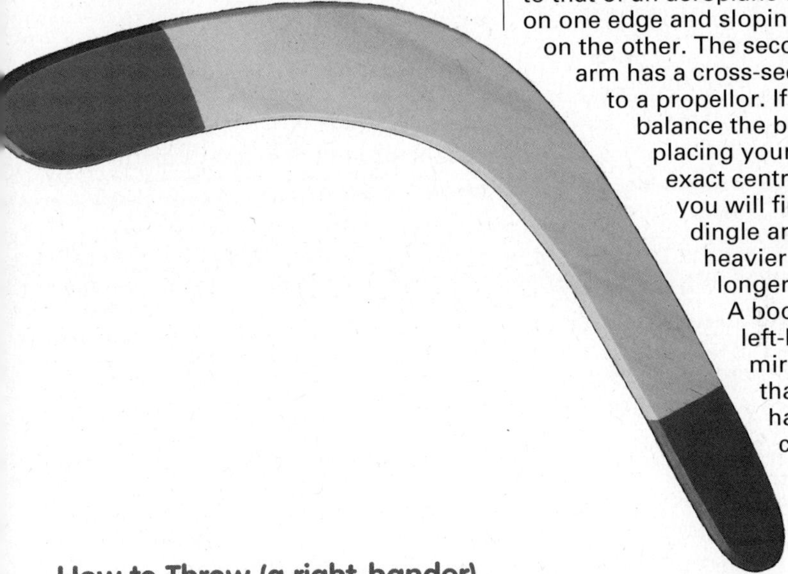

The Arms

These are quite different. On the dingle arm the cross-section is similar to that of an aeroplane's wing: blunt on one edge and sloping to a taper on the other. The second or lifting arm has a cross-section similar to a propellor. If you try to balance the boomerang by placing your finger at the exact centre of the bend, you will find that the dingle arm is slightly heavier and a little longer.

A boomerang for a left-hander is the mirror image of that of a right-hander, and circles in the opposite direction.

How to Throw (a right-hander)

1 Place about 4 cm of the rounded side of the dingle arm (this arm gives better precision when throwing) on your palm between the thumb and the first finger. Close these firmly on it.

2 Incline the boomerang on about a 60° plane to the horizon.

3 The boomerang should be thrown directly outward towards the horizon and not aimed up in the sky. Aim at a point about a hundred metres away and two to three metres high, holding the boomerang behind your head.

4 The "throw" is critical. The boomerang is not actually thrown, but forced out of the hand with a special movement that gives it the all important spin. This involves a flick (not a twist) of the wrist downwards, and at the same moment a tightening of the grip on the boomerang with the thumb and first and second fingers.
As the boomerang end is rounded, the tightening of the grasp makes the fingers slide down post the end, sending it flying.

How to Catch

1 The safest, easiest and least painful way to catch the boomerang in mid-air is to "clap" it between the open palms.

2 It can be caught with one hand but this is more difficult and harder on the knuckles. It is done by grasping at the exact middle of the boomerang when it is in a slow hover.

How to Control a Flying Boomerang

Boomerangs must not be thrown in a wind of over 5 kilometres! They are deadly weapons. Go fly a kite!

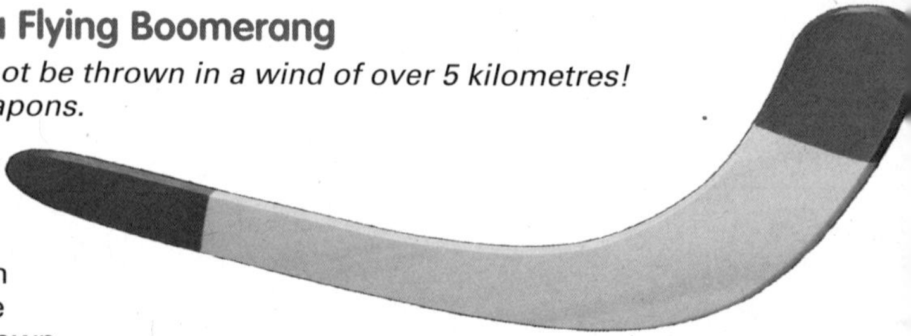

a If there is no breeze at all, it does not matter in what direction the boomerang is thrown.
b Elevation: this is controlled by the angle of the plane of the boomerang and the horizon. 60° is about right, but if it does not go high enough and touches the ground before returning, flatten this up to about 45°. If it goes too high, steepen it up to 75°.
c Safety: once the boomerang leaves the thrower's hand there is no way of calling it back.

Musts for Boomerang Throwing

a A very gentle breeze or no wind at all.
b A large empty field. Screaming children, hurt spectators and owners of cars with broken windows are no fun. Remember: skill is more important than brute force.
c Practice brings skill.
d Lifting your arm the day after your first throws may be impossible if you practice for too long.

Care and Maintenance

a A chipped boomerang can be mended with a good epoxy resin glue and sanded down smoothly.
b Keep pressed flat when not in use. Guard against excessive heat and moisture.
c A highly polished boomerang goes best. Use either a 50 : 50 mixture of ski wax and goanna oil or waterproof brown boot polish.

Note:
Boomerangs can be made out of a fine five-ply marine plywood.
The following firms make boomerangs in Australia:
- Hawes Boomerangs, P.O. Box 5, Mudgeeraba, Queensland, Australia.
- Wycheproof Boomerangs, 380 Broadway, Wycheproof, Victoria, Australia 3527.

see also Boomerangs; Kooris

Bunyips

The bunyip is an animal living in swamps and river backwaters in the Australian bush and forest areas. It is seldom seen but very much feared. The Kooris, the first people to live in Australia, stay away from areas where bunyips live. They are very afraid of the terribly loud roars the animal makes when it is interrupted or angry.
There are several descriptions of the bunyip. These include looking like a hippopotamus with scales on its back, a round-headed and long-necked creature with the tail and body of an ox, and an alligator with a horse-like body.
During the nineteenth century a variety of people reported seeing bunyips. French explorers on the Swan River in the south of Western Australia wrote in their report that they had seen a bunyip. Sometimes convicts, prisoners sent out from England to Australia, escaped and lived for a long time in the bush with the Kooris. One of these told people he met later that he had seen bunyips. Others were farmers and travelling priests. No bunyips have been seen at Bunyip River

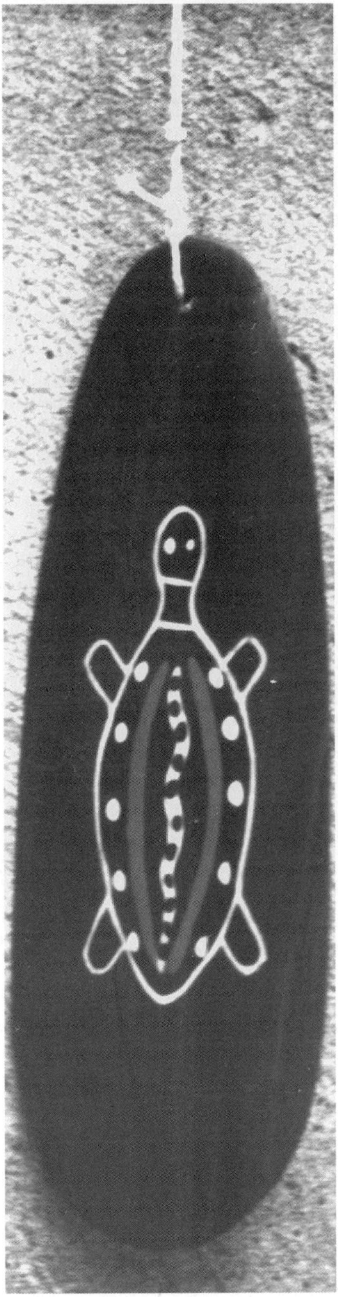

near Melbourne, but early settlers are reported to have heard loud roars from the direction of the river at night sometimes. Zoologists have never found any parts of bunyips, although some Kooris pointed out several large fossilized bones to a farmer, Mr Westgarth, in the 1840s as bones of the bunyip.
There is another theory that the sound of the bunyip was really the sound of the bull-roarer. This was a specially shaped piece of wood on a rope that had religious meaning for its Koori owner. When a special ceremony was to be held, the bullroarer was swung around the owner's head quickly in circles. This made a terrible noise and was to keep away women and people not belonging to the tribe who were not allowed to see the ceremony. This may explain the sound of the bunyip, but no one can explain the animals people have seen and called bunyips.
Around the 1850s in Sydney, "bunyip" was used to refer to a nuisance or impostor.

see also Animals; Kooris

Bushfires

Bushfires make anyone who has lived in Australia worried. These are the fires which burn uncontrolled in the bush and forest areas. As Australia is the driest continent and often has droughts, bushfires are a huge problem. Many lives are lost and areas of farmland and bush are burnt, often each summer, because of bushfires. In the typical long, hot and dry Australian summers, conditions in the bush made up of mainly eucalyptus trees make the danger of bushfires very high. When there have been several wet years with good growing seasons, the undergrowth, the bush and grass growing close to the ground, is thick. The next dry summer dries this out and if it catches fire it burns and spreads quickly. Once started, a fire is difficult to control and hundreds of square kilometres of bush can be destroyed.

The most dangerous of bushfires is the crown fire. The crowns or tree tops of the eucalypts are thickly covered with leaves full of oil. The fire literally jumps from crown to crown. It no longer burns normally but consists of a series of explosions as the oil in the eucalyptus leaves on the crown explodes and bursts into flames. Burning branches and whole trees crash to the ground in an inferno. The only possible escape for any creature is to go into a large, deep body of water such as a river. The difficulty is that these are not very common in the bush in a dry summer.

Many lives and huge numbers of properties and animals have been lost during bushfires. Over the Christmas/New Year period in 1966-1967 a bushfire near Hobart in Tasmania was out of control for days. Within the burnt-out area, sixty-two people were killed and 1,400 homes were destroyed. The worst fires ever were in summer 1994 around Sydney. Most of the fire-fighting is done by volunteers who join a local branch of "The Country Fire Authority".

Prevention of bushfires is important. This includes public education programs with roadside signs and information for school children. Fire towers are built within large areas of eucalyptus forest at regular intervals and fire-watchers are there all summer.

Although large areas are often damaged by fire, the Australian bush re-grows quite quickly, and much faster than European forests. Eucalyptus trees have developed certain characteristics that make sure they grow again after fire. Along the branches at regular intervals are hidden or concealed buds of new leaves. These buds are so well covered that fire seldom burns them. After a fire they develop very quickly and new green leaves grow directly out from the tree trunk.

see also Artesian Water; Eucalypts and Gum Trees; Rain Making; Outback Life; Voluntary Welfare

Camels

The only wild camels in the world, "camelus dromedarius", are found in Australia in the desert areas, particularly in Central Australia. They were brought into the country by the Afghans or "Ghans", the Australian name for people from the tribes of South East Afghanistan and North West Pakistan. The Ghans first arrived in 1860 as camel drivers and were very important in opening up inland Australia. Camels made it possible to transport heavy loads for long distances through the desert and semi-desert areas without great problems of water. They helped in rescue work in the desert and in exploring the large dry areas of the inland. Camels were very important when railways were laid and when the Overland Telegraph line was built. This line, completed in 1872, went from Adelaide on the south coast for over 2,000 kilometres to Darwin on the north coast. This telegraph system made quick contact and immediate exchange of news with the rest of the world possible. Up to this time a sailing-ship needed at least six weeks in one direction to deliver news and letters. Camels made it possible to construct this communication system fifty years before trucks and planes could have been used, as most of the area it goes through is desert. Regular work that camels were used for were carrying supplies and mail to outback cattle and sheep stations and in helping setting up water pumps and bores. Without the Ghans and their camels, inland Australia could not have been opened up for settlement.

The original train running from Alice Springs to Adelaide was called "The Ghan" after these men, their camels and the important work they did, and one of the new trains has taken over this name.

About 3,000 Afghan camel drivers came to Australia between 1860 and 1930. They kept their traditional way of life, living in "Ghan Towns" they built next to main towns. They kept their religion, and the mullahs, their religious leaders, could be heard calling the people to prayer at the standard times.

The development and introduction of cars and trucks in the outback in the 1920s slowly but surely took over the jobs the camels had done. The Afghans who stayed in Australia worked mainly in the outback in farming and running general stores, shops where everything can be bought. As there was no more work for their camels, they let them free. These groups grew larger over the years and were the beginning of the wild camel herds in the Australian outback.
Today visitors are often surprised to see many camels running free in the drier areas. One problem the large number of wild camels brings is erosion. The vegetation in Central Australia is very fragile, and the concentration of the camel's weight on the relatively small area of its feet disturbs the sandy soil surface and plant life. Plant life and the ecosystem in the desert is very delicate or fragile and easily damaged because of the low rainfall, extreme temperatures and wind. The kangaroo, in contrast, has its weight spread over a larger foot area and does not cause this problem. On the other hand, these camels are known to be very healthy and are able to be exported to the Middle East. Some wild camels are rounded up and sold directly. Others are used for breeding and kept on farms for future sales for export.

see also Farming; Immigration; Northern Territory; Outback Life; Settlement of Australia; Journeys Inland

Cattlemen in Choppers

A cattle station is the Australian name for a very large farm for cattle. In the "Top End" or the north and north-west of Australia, cattle stations are huge. Two examples of large cattle stations are Wave Hill and Victoria River Downs. Both stretch over 12.5 thousand square kilometres. The country in this area is generally flat with small outcrops of rocks, some low hills and creeks or small river beds which only fill during the wet season. Tall seasonal grass covers a lot of the plains and the bush consists mainly of thick low shrubs with small gum or eucalyptus trees. It is excellent cattle country and cattle are an important industry in Australia. Although the country is good, there are difficult jobs for the station owners. Some of these are mustering or finding the cattle from the large open areas, sorting them into groups for selling or keeping, checking them for disease, and sending them to the market. They have to be kept in good condition for selling. Previously mustering was done by stockmen, the men who look after the cattle, riding special stock horses and having specially trained cattle dogs. Today the stockmen are helped by helicopters or "choppers" which do most of the work. The number of cattle eight stockmen on horseback can bring into the yards in three or four weeks can be done by one chopper in a day. The pilots are highly skilled at manœuvring and low flying and take many risks. When the pilots work later in the season, the ground is so dry that a lot of dust is raised by the cattle as they move. This can make it difficult for them to see clearly and there is more danger.

The advantages the choppers have are their speed and the way they can move. These two skills mean that they can find the cattle and move them together much quicker than men on horseback.
To be successful the pilots must be skilled at flying.
It is also necessary to have an excellent knowledge of cattle and the country, or the bush or outback as the Australians call it, that the cattle are in. Most pilots are bushmen who were born in the bush.
During the season, "the dry", from March to November, the choppers work six days a week, flying from just after dawn till the late afternoon. Often jobs take many days and the pilots sleep out in the open as the stockmen on horseback always did.

see also Farming; Sheep

Convicts

During the 18th and 19th centuries in Britain one of the common forms of punishment for breaking the law was transportation. Prisons were so full in England and the British wanted to send bad people out of the country. Prisoners sent to another country by ship were called "convicts". After the War of Independence, America did not let Britain send any more convicts. Prisons soon filled and something had to be done with the prisoners. This was one of the main reasons the British decided to settle in Australia. Until that time Australia had not been interesting as a place to live in. There were no suitable goods, such as spices, for trade, the climate was much hotter and drier than in Europe and the vegetation was very different. No Europeans had shown interest in the country. However, the problem of prisoners was a very big one for the British and the decision was made to start a colony in Australia.

The First Fleet of eleven sailing-ships with 1,500 people including about 800 convicts left England under Governor Phillip in May 1787. It arrived at Botany Bay near Sydney on 18 January 1788. Food supplies for the first two years were carried as it was not expected that the colony could supply itself within a short time.
A settlement was built north of Botany Bay at Port Jackson, today Sydney Harbour.
During the next eighty years more than 160,000 convicts were transported. Convicts had to stay for either 7 years, 14 years or their whole life in prison. Most convicts came from cities. The normal convict was poor, uneducated and had often done something against the law although this was often just stealing a loaf of bread. The bad social conditions in England and the extreme punishments for crimes at those times need to be known before saying that all the convicts were bad by nature. For many it was a matter of life or death and the fight for food. Those convicted of serious crimes were normally hung, not transported. A small number of educated men, especially political prisoners, were also among the convicts. The group of political prisoners were people who had organised and been in strikes and demonstrations against so many people being poor and unemploy-ment. There were many Irish and Scotsmen who did not like the English.
The handling of convicts was very different, depending on the time they were sent out, their crime, their behaviour and those in control. Up until 1820 Governor Macquarie's ideas were used. These were that people who had not had a good start and a fair chance in life could return to the right way if controlled carefully and given a chance. The government authorities had very little housing for convicts and they were not usually locked in to the prisons at night. Many worked for the government and were free to work for themselves after three o'clock in the afternoon.

Others were sent to work for free settlers as servants or farm workers on new farms. A convict had the chance of freedom before his time if he behaved well. A "ticket of leave" freed him and let him work for himself under certain conditions.
A "conditional pardon" made him free as long as he did not return to Britain. Until 1820 freed convicts were often given land and tools to help start a farm.
The system became much worse after an enquiry in 1820. This said that conditions were too good for convicts and ex-convicts. The result of the report was protests in Britain which caused bad changes.
Generally, conditions were made worse and there were more chain gangs where prisoners were chained together by the feet. They had to walk and work with these chains. Special prison settlements with very bad conditions and terrible punishments were also set up by the British in Tasmania and on Norfolk Island.
Various factors brought an end to the convict era. Free settlers did not like the convicts as they were cheap

workers for the landowners.
A landowner would take a cheap convict before he would pay more for a free worker. Free convicts wanted to stop discrimination against them and strong criticism of the terrible handling of convicts came from Australia and Britain. In London, a committee from the House of Commons for the British Government decided that as many prisoners expected better conditions in Australia than in England, transportation was not effective.
From 1840 convict numbers dropped and transportation was finally stopped in 1868.

Records of Male Transports

Name	Age	Trade	Status	Crime	Sentence
Ashford, John	33	labourer	widower	stealing sheep	15 years
Bywater, Robert	18	roper	single	theft	14 years
Edwards, Joseph	38	labourer	married, 6 children.	theft	10 years
Keats, Benjamin	25	weaver	married, 1 child	stealing fowls	14 years

The records of female convicts show that women were often deported because of "disorderly conduct" and, of course, for the same reasons as the male convicts, that is for stealing.

Source: G. Simsons, using Government records from the Archives Office of Tasmania,

see also Settlement of Australia

Dingoes

The "dingo" or "warragal" is the Australian wild dog. These are the names the Kooris, the first Australians, gave it. It has been in Australia for about ten thousand years. It is like the modern dogs but there are certain differences. The dingo is usually a brownish-yellow colour, a little lighter on the chest and with some white on its tail and feet. When it moves it lopes, that is to run in a steady and relaxed way, not like common dogs. The dingoes' ears have a definite point, are curved like a wolf's and always stand up. They never bark but howl and have larger feet and teeth than other dogs. Pure dingoes sometimes hunt in groups of two or three especially when bad conditions make it necessary to hunt larger animals. They also make small groups at mating time. Adults not old enough to be parents help look after the pups. Apart from these situations, pure dingoes usually live alone, having a favourite area and not moving far from this. A typical dingo is 1.85 metres long including 35 cm of tail.

In general dingoes have a bad name. However, studies show that they do not deserve this bad name. They are not aggressive in general. Other people who have kept them as pets have also found them to be the same as other pet dogs. Dingoes eat mainly small mammals, especially rabbits. Rabbits are a huge problem for farmers as they eat grass and damage the roots so that it takes a long time to re-grow and there is less for the sheep to eat. In some areas of New South Wales and Queensland rabbits and wild pigs have become a great problem when dingoes have been hunted.

The dingo plays an important part in farm life in an indirect way that many people do not know about. The two important kinds of working dogs, the Australian cattle dog and the Australian kelpie which works mainly with sheep, have dingo blood in them.

see also Animals; Farming; Kooris; Rabbits; Sheep

Dreamtime

The dreamtime or dreaming is individual and very personal for every Koori, the first Australian inhabitants. They all have their own dreaming which gives their life meaning, both spiritually and in their daily life. The dreaming goes back to the time when the Kooris' ancestors were creating the world as they know it today. Before creation the earth is described in Koori legends as a huge, flat disc floating in space. There was no life – no people, birds, animals or plants. The land was flat, without rivers, valleys, hills or oceans. The dreaming describes how the land was formed and living things were created. Legends of the dreamtime are different from tribe to tribe and include all birds, animals and physical features such as hills and rivers of the Australian continent. The most important stories are, however, those which give rules about how individuals and groups should behave. These rules must be followed as they make sure that the society runs without problems. For tens of thousands of years these rules have been passed down from generation to generation by Koori story-tellers. The dreamtime gives each person security – it explains their exact place in society and the physical and social world. These laws are set and never change and include rights, responsibilities, who it is possible to marry and where it is possible to live. The dreamtime is very detailed and complicated. Chess is said to be a child's game in comparison to the details and rules of the dreamtime.

Each Koori has a special bird or animal totem and is not allowed to hunt or eat this. There are certain legends about each totem which relates to the Koori personally and make a special place for the individual person in life. These legends may be repeated in dances. These dances themselves are part of the dreaming, joining the past to their life today in a dimension of life that does not seem to exist in the West European's experience. A spirit never dies but is re-incarnated with a new child. This connects each person strongly to his past and his environment. The tjuringas symbolise the dreaming for the Kooris. These are very special sacred stones and often represent the owner's totem animal or his spirit. The stones are pear-shaped, oval or round and may have the tracks of animals or birds or designs of lines and circles cut into them. Charcoal or red ochre is often used to colour them. Some tribes make wooden tjuringas which they also use as bullroarers. The name "bullroarer" comes from the noise they make when tied to a piece of string and swung in circles around the head. This noise was used to keep unwanted people away from sacred ceremonies and areas. Bullroarer is the European name. The wooden tjuringas are much larger than the stone ones and can measure twenty by one hundred centimetres. These are also decorated and have spiritual importance to the owners.

Two Legends from the Dreaming

Purra – The Cloud

In the dreamtime, Purra was a man travelling around the country looking for a wife. Everywhere he went he was a stranger and so no one was willing to give a daughter to him. As he got old he got ugly and one day on his travels he went to have a drink at a waterhole. At the water he saw his reflection and knew he now had no chance to find a wife. This made him so angry that he decided to punish everyone who had not given him their daughter. He made a big bark bucket and began to collect all the water from the country so that everyone would have difficulties and problems from this just as he had had from being lonely. However, Kubelin, the Thunder Man, who had a very loud voice saw him and called to everyone. His voice was so strong that it travelled all over the country. The men chased Purra with their spears but he flew up into the sky and changed himself into a cloud with his bucket full of water. Kunbabin, the Lightning Man, was the best spear fighter in the country and he jumped into the air and threw his spear. It flew like a flash of lightning and made a hole in Purra's bucket. The water fell to the earth in a huge downfall of rain. Kunbabin changed himself into lightning and decided to live in the sky and Kubelin also went to live there. Both of them live very high and cannot be seen.
Kubelin keeps a watch and whenever Purra begins to fill his bucket with water, he thunders a warning and calls Kunbabin, who sends his lightning spear to hit the bucket and bring rain and the water back to the earth.

see also Kooris; Bunyips

The Black Swans

In the dreamtime there were only white swans. During this time two were flying along the north coast of the continent. They landed on a lagoon, but did not know it belonged to the eagles. The eagles were very angry and attacked the swans. They tore out most of the swan's feathers, carried them to the south and dropped them in the desert. The swans lay dying but then a flock of black crows came flying across the sky. Each crow let one of its black feathers fall down onto the swans as a present to help them grow strong and be clothed. When the swans were better, they flew on south. Today they are covered with the black feathers of the crows except for the blood on their beaks and the white feathers on the ends of their wing. These remind them that the eagles are still their enemies.

Economic History

Since European settlement in Australia in 1788 many changes have been made. The land has been developed for settlement and farming. Dams for storing water have been built so that during the dry summers and long dry drought periods there is enough water for the population and some farms. As well, mineral resources such as coal, iron, and gold have been developed. All these are necessary for the growing population.

At first, the huge, newly discovered continent did not have any type of transport system such as roads or railways. There were also no communication systems such as the post office. Both these were necessary for life and business as the British knew it. Particular problems were the transport system because of the huge distances and water storage facilities due to the dry climate.

The Beginning: 1788 to 1820

The convicts and civilians who arrived with the First Fleet were only interested in surviving. They needed all their energy to get to know the new climate and conditions to grow crops and fruit trees, and to keep animals. This was a long, slow process and it was not until 1805 that wool was ready for export, the first Australian export product. John Macarthur developed a special breed of merino sheep which produced fine wool and lived well in the hot dry climate and on the hard ground. The other main difficulty was enough land for farming around Sydney. The mountains behind the city were like a wall stopping people going further. This was not solved until 1813 when the Blue Mountains were finally crossed and the open country on the other side could be used for more farming.

The Farming Age: 1820 to 1851

The Industrial Revolution in Britain led to a huge demand for raw materials. Sheep farming, being very profitable, increased quickly after 1813 and the "unlocking" or opening of the land behind Sydney. Farmers and those hoping to be farmers who wanted land did not listen to the government. It had only certain small areas where people could live and have farms. People wanting to start new farms were to wait until the local and English governments decided on how to sell the land, who to sell it to, and the price. These new farmers did not wait. They moved out into new, unexplored areas and "squatted", that is stopped and set up camps where the land was good and had permanent water. If things went well, they built a house and other buildings needed for farming. In general, wool was the most important product. On a smaller but still important scale, South Australia and Tasmania produced sufficient wheat for export.

The Goldrush and the Boom: 1851 to 1890

Gold was first discovered in 1823. The government did not publish this information because it was afraid of what would happen to the new colony if it became known.

The goldrush first began in Victoria in 1851. This was the start of very big changes in Australia. The population grew, there was more building and businesses began. The population rose from around half a million in 1851 to 1.7 million in 1871 and in this period over 50,000,000 ounces (over 140 tonnes) of gold were mined. With more money from the gold and more people, the government also had more money. This was spent on roads, railways and government services, for example. Now Australia did not need money from the British parliament. Private investment was also high. There were many new buildings and industry grew.

The Depression, Recovery, World War I and After (1890-1939)

In 1890 there was a bad economic depression. The large economic problems in Britain were also felt in Australia. This showed that she was still strongly dependent economically on Britain. Wool prices fell, land prices in Melbourne collapsed and there was a banking crisis in 1893. Unemployment rose and the Shearers' Strike, though not successful at the time was very important for the new trade unions in Australia. The sheep population fell from over one million in 1891 to half a million by 1902. The situation was made worse by a long, hard drought from 1895 to 1902. This was a disaster for a country "riding on the sheep's back".

The economy slowly improved after 1900. More gold-mining, refrigerated shipping which meant that meat could be exported, railways and better sheep and shearing equipment were the main reasons. There were good and bad periods during this time. British migrants arrived and the government gave money for irrigation schemes. This meant that farms had water all year and could

produce more. Local manufacturing industries such as cars, clothing and electrical goods grew. Taxes on imports to make them cost more kept the local industries in business. However, the country suffered greatly with the world economic depression.

World War II to 1972

Economically, World War II made Australia develop local manufacturing industries as Europe could no longer provide her needs. In general, this was a time when everyone had a job and a good living standard. The immigration program brought skilled and unskilled workers to Australia. Local and international investment brought progress. Wheat and wool prices were high and there were many technical changes in industry bringing higher productivity. This situation began to change towards the end of the 1960s.
It was made worse by the start of the European Economic Community, as Europe, especially Britain, was one of Australia's main markets.
The situation was helped only by mining, especially the export of minerals and iron to Japan.

1971 to Today

The economic situation has continued to worsen since the early 1970s. Inflation was between 11% and 14% for many years, although this fell to below 2% in 1992*. Unemployment rose steeply to over 10% in 1983, fell but then increased again**.

* In 1996 it was 1.5%.

** It was 8.6% in January 1997.

see also Farming; Immigration; Journeys Inland; Sheep; Southern Cross

Electric Stingrays

Stingrays are a type of fish. They are large, flat and look like a round disc with a head at the front and a long fine tail at the back. The thin flaps at the sides are large and give the stingray its round shape. By moving these flaps, the ray moves itself through the water. The tail is the dangerous part. It can give a very painful sting.
Stingrays are found throughout the oceans of the world. The special kind of stingrays, "torpediniformes", is only found along the Australian coasts from Western Australia to Southern Queensland.

These stingrays are small, growing only to 60 cm in length. However, they can produce an electric shock varying from 8 to 22 volts. The parts which makes the electricity are like muscles and run along the edges of both sides of the body from the eyes to the last gill or opening for breathing. Shocks are made when a stingray attacks a fish it wants to kill or when it is fighting off enemies. The strength of the electric shock falls if the ray uses it often and quickly, and it takes some time for it to re-charge. The record shock was felt by twelve people standing in a line holding hands.

see also Animals

Eucalypts or Gum Trees

The kind of plant, the "eucalyptus", is native only to Australia and islands to the north. The trees are commonly called "gums" and make up about 95% of all forest and bushland vegetation in Australia. The trees have evolved over ten million years alone because Australia has been cut off from other land for this time. From a distance, a eucalpytus forest is blue. This is because oil is given off from the leaves into the air, and the light shining through this looks blue. A gum forest has a soft, rounded silhouette in direct contrast to pine forests. This round shape is because the leaves fall in groups from the branches. The leaves are long, fine and silver grey-green in colour. They have developed over thousands of years to grow well in the local conditions, especially the long, hot, dry summers. Unlike most other trees, the leaves normally hang down towards the ground so that the sun can reach both sides. This position lets the leaves turn slowly back and forth as the sun moves. Therefore, when it is hot, only the edge catches the sun's direct rays and the strong heat. The silver-grey colouring of the leaves also reflects off the heat. Both these factors mean less loss of water and help the tree to live in the hot climate.
The Greek word "eu-kalyptos" means well-covered. It describes the little cap or hat which covers each flower bud. This covers the small flower in a strong, hard, waterproof container as it grows. The gum or eucalyptus flowers are normally small, only one or two centimetres across. As they often grow in large groups, the trees are completely covered in white, cream, yellow, pink or red in the flowering season. There are more than five hundred species of eucalypts. Eucalyptus oil is produced from the leaves. This oil has different perfumes and the strongest comes from the peppermint gum. The perfume can be best smelt in the bush after rain. It also smells very strong in a summer heat wave after several days of around 40°C.
The perfume stays and the air is full of the oil that the heat has taken out of the leaves. It feels like the air would explode if a fire were lighted. Eucalypts are very different and grow in many areas. The snow gum, growing in the Australian Alps, lives with winter temperatures below zero and snow.
Other types of eucalypts include ghost gums, which have a smooth, straight trunk with silver-white bark that looks ghost-like at night. There is also the river redgum which is a huge tree with huge, wide branches that grows in rivers and does not rot in water. The mountain ash eucalypt is the tallest hardwood tree in the world after the Californian redwood tree which grows in the U.S.A. One mountain ash eucalpyt in Tasmania has a diameter of 14 metres, is over 100 metres high and the first branch does not grow until 70 metres up the tree. It is between 300 and 350 years old. There are also only five types of eucalyptus trees that the koala can live from. This is one reason why it is not found everywhere in Australia and certain areas have to be kept for it to live in.

see also Animals; Bushfires; Food; Kooris; National Parks

Explorers

William Dampier was an English seaman who lived from 1652 to 1715. He was the first Englishman to land in Australia. It was because of bad luck and some bad decisions that he is not remembered as the man who claimed the country for England.
In 1688, the "Cygnet", the ship he was sailing on, stopped at the north-west coast near today's town of Dampier. While the ship was being repaired, he found time to explore the country close to it. As he did this he made notes on the way of life of the Kooris, the first Australians. In the book he wrote about his travels and Australia, he said the country was very dry and did not have many trees, grass and other plants. He also said the people were very primitive.
Although what Dampier saw was not very helpful for England, he wanted to return and find out more about the country. After taking a lot of time talking to the English government, they gave him a ship. In 1699 he sailed from England. He hoped to land on the east coast and find something important for England. He had problems such as heavy storms which blew him off his course he wanted to sail and his ship was in a bad condition. This meant he could only sail along parts of the west and north coasts of Australia. On this second trip Dampier also did not find anything good for trade or good land for farming. Because of his reports the British were not interested in Australia. It was nearly a hundred years before they were.
In 1768 **Captain James Cook** sailed to Tahiti to watch the planet Venus crossing the sun. He was then to sail further west-south-west to explore the South Pacific Ocean. He found and made maps of New Zealand and the east coast of Australia. In general, he made a realistic report about Australia. The country was fertile and a lot of food could be produced in contrast to the land Dampier had seen. Cook's reports of the Koori people were very different from those of other Europeans. He wrote about their great knowledge and understanding of the natural environment and how this was linked to their way of life.

see also Australia – Areas and Regions; Journeys Inland; Kooris;
New Zealand – Areas and Regions;
Settlement of Australia

Famous and Influential People

Arthur Calwell (1896 to 1973) was one of the Labour Party's leaders. The Labour Party is one of the two main political parties in Australian politics. He held seats in parliament from 1940 to 1972 and was a minister in the cabinet while Labour was in power in the forties. The important change he made for Australia was during 1945 to 1949 when he was Minister for Immigration. At this time he introduced the phrase, "Populate or perish!". The basic philosophy behind this slogan was that Australia needed more of her area settled and a higher population. This was necessary to protect herself from being taken over by another nation and, in general, to develop a modern economy. Arthur Calwell was responsible for the design and implementation of Australia's immigration program after World War II. Begun in 1946, the program aimed at bringing 70,000 immigrants annually to Australia by 1948. Each person payed only £10 for the trip by ship, the government payed the rest. The Australian population was 7.5 million in 1947. The immigration schemes' success in populating the country is clear from the example of 1952 when 170,000 people arrived. The population reached about 8.5 million by 1951, a 13.3% increase and 10.5 million by 1961, a 40% increase in the 14 years.

Albert Namatjira was born near Alice Springs in Central Australia in 1902 and died in 1959. He was a Koori, one of the first Australians. His water colour paintings of the Australian outback are still well-liked today and show the Koori view of the Australian inland using European water-colour painting techniques. The paintings have a certain style and use definite colours. The air and heat of the inland create blues, purples and all shades of pink. These tones are very strong at dawn and dusk and at these times the trees, hills and landscape change to these colours. During the early morning and late afternoon the sunlight brings out the very deep browns, oranges, yellows and reds of the sandy soil and rocky outcrops, often in contrast to the white trunks of the ghost gums. These are the colours Namatjira often used in his paintings, and they are still typical of Koori landscape painters today. The pictures are realistic, and each rock or tree has its definite shape. Many of his paintings were of different parts of the MacDonnel Ranges just north of Ayer's Rock, and include Alice Springs. One of his very famous paintings is of the twin ghost gums which can still be seen west of Alice Springs, and were on a special stamp from the Australian Post Office.

Dame Nellie Melba was born as Helen Porter Mitchell and lived from 1861 to 1931. She was a soprano and one of the most famous of all times.

Her home city was Melbourne and this was where she took her singing name from.
Her Italian music teacher persuaded her to make opera singing her career and she sailed to London with her father in 1886. She sang in Paris, Brussels, St Petersburg and finally all over Europe and in the U.S.A. In 1889 she began singing in Covent Garden, London, and did so every season for many years. There were twenty-five operas she sang during her career. Her voice was described by critics as beautiful, powerful and even, and it can be heard on some early records. After 1909, she spent her time in both Europe and Australia, making her final appearance in 1926 in London. Returning to Australia, she lived in Sydney but she was buried near Melbourne.

Caroline Chisholm was born in Northhampton, England in 1808. In 1838 she moved to New South Wales in Australia with her husband and two sons. Always having helped taking care of others, the problems migrants, especially single women, were having on arrival in Australia worried her very much. When her husband returned to his work in India in 1840, she stayed in Sydney. There she opened a "Female Immigrants Home" in an old army building on Circular Quay, a part of Sydney Harbour. In the five years after this she looked after 11,000 people.
The main problems were finding jobs for young women, and work and housing for men and their families in the country. Because she cared so much she often travelled long distances. This was normally done with groups of young women and girls to the country towns to look for good and safe jobs for them. Her work stopped social problems and unemployment in crowded Sydney.
In 1845 Caroline Chisholm returned to England to join her husband who was retiring from India. The couple opened an office in London to help migrants travelling to New South Wales. Again in 1854 she travelled with migrants to Australia.
At this time she had the support of important and powerful people such as Charles Dickens. This time she travelled through the gold-fields to look at the situation there.
On the gold-fields she organised accommodation for travellers just arriving. After this she moved to Sydney and started a girls' school.
In 1866 she and her husband returned to England because they were not well. She died in 1877, poor and no longer important or even remembered by the public. Her gravestone at Northhampton has the words "The emigrant's friend" written on it. It does not mention that her husband is buried with her and that they both shared most of the work done for the new settlers to Australia.

see also Food; Immigration; Kooris; Politics; Uluru and the Red Centre

Farming

One of the first and often most lasting impressions visitors to Australia have is that of space and distance. There is so much land. Therefore, there are many different types of **farming** where the climate and the land make this possible. One of the main differences between Australian and European farming is the intensity. In Europe every corner of a farm is used, but on Australian farms the areas left unfarmed around fences, roads and buildings are large and there is quite often land that is not always used. Although there is this difference between Australian and European farming, one example of Australian farming that could be compared to a normal European farm is an irrigated rice farm of 300 hectares. This is quite a small farm and is often run by one full-time farmer with some part-time help from his wife or a farm worker. At planting or harvesting time one or two other people will probably help by driving tractors on the farm or taking the harvest to the storage or sales depot. The other type of farming in Australia is extensive where a farm, or station as it is called, is many hundreds of square kilometres, the animals have large areas to move in and are often only looked at by the station workers a few times a year.

The Kooris, the first Australians, harvested the small amount of natural grass. There were no grasses which produced large quantities of seeds, and there were many different fruits and vegetables to harvest as well as animals and fish to catch. The Kooris could live well except in bad drought years and did not need to have farms. When the First Fleet arrived in Australia with the first European people, growing crops, fruit trees and vegetables was most important as they did not have much with them. England was too far away to be able to send them food regularly, so farming was very necessary. Once the land had been explored and opened up and farmers began to know and understand the climate and land, farming became very important. It was the main basis for trade with other countries, especially wool and wheat. For many years Australia was "carried on the sheeps' back" because the high quality, fine merino wool was needed by England and Europe for the clothing industry. Once refrigeration was developed, meat was also sold and shipped to Europe.

The Australian **wine industry** began with the first settlement. Australian wine was sent to England in 1822 and won a prize in a competition. Different people have grown grapes for wine production during Australia's history. One example is in the Barossa Valley, north of Adelaide, where there is a mediterranean climate similar to southern Italy. At first there were many problems as the vines often died because of diseases and the hot, dry climate. It was also necessary to find out how the different climate and soil affected the taste and quality of the grapes. In Europe, for example, stones are often put on the ground around the wines to keep the heat. In Australia the roots of the plants need to be kept cooler. Very often wines will be made from grapes from two areas – those from irrigated areas for the amount of liquid and those from dry area farms for the flavour. 'Moppity Park' is a dry area farm with vineyards near Young in New South Wales. Some grapes from Moppity Park are used with grapes of an irrigated vineyard in the region to produce an excellent Australian wine. Wine is produced in many areas of Australia today. It is becoming more popular with Australians than before and some is successfully exported.

Market gardens are near every large city and town and are market gardens which grow fruit and vegetables for the local market. However, Queensland, the north-eastern state has a warm, moist climate and therefore has a long growing period. During the winter and months of the year when vegetables do not grow outside in the cooler southern states, many fresh vegetables are sent by road and rail from Queensland. The variety and freshness is excellent, and the contrast in quality with hot-house vegetables is large. The warm tropical and sub-tropical climate on the east coast of Queensland makes it an excellent area for growing tropical fruits such as mangoes, pawpaws, bananas, pineapples, passion-fruit and avocadoes. The climate is also good for sugar cane which is grown in large areas.

The **dairy** and **cheese industry** is in the more southern states. Milking cows are kept to supply the local markets with milk, butter, cream, cheese and other dairy products. European cheese makers are being looked for by Australian farmers and businessmen who want to build up the industry. These people would come to live in Australia and work in new factories. They would bring the skills to make cheeses using the Australian milk and know what changes are necessary to make in process and how to make these. The number of cheeses being made is increasing, but is not very wide compared to the varieties produced in Europe.

Sheep and **cattle** are kept on smaller farms of 200 to 500 hectares in the wetter areas, but most are kept on large dry area stations. These are often hundreds of square kilometres and often carry only one animal to the square kilometre because of the low rainfall and very little vegetation. Cattle on these stations are kept for meat and the sheep for meat and wool.

see also Australia – Areas and Regions; Camels; Cattlemen in Choppers; Dingoes; Economic History; Kooris; Rabbits; Sheep

Flightless Birds (NZ)

New Zealand has many birds, including many which are flightless. Seven species are in danger of dying out. The **takahe**, a ground bird, thought to be no longer living was surprisingly re-discovered in 1948. The takahe is the size of a hen with dark black-blue feathers and a large, bright red beak. It lives in the south-west of the South Island in the mountains west of Lake Te Anau. In summer it lives in the snow-grass areas of the marshes and streams. In winter it goes down to the native beech forests for protection from the snow and cold, and for food. The bird is well-known because it has "come back from the dead" and a chance to save a bird from dying out is rare.

The **kiwi** is small, round and brown-grey. As it is a nocturnal or night bird it is difficult to watch. It has a very bad temper, and when things upset it, it often kicks them. Kiwis are rather

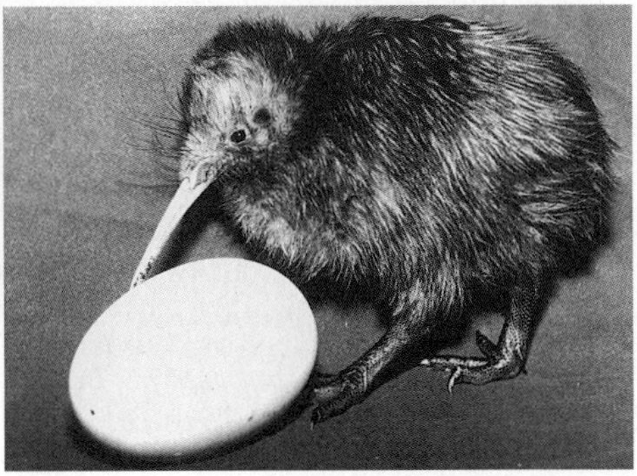

lazy, sleeping up to twenty hours a day. They live on worms which they find by smell. Their nostrils are on the end of a long, fine curved bill, which they push into the earth. They live in burrows, the female laying an egg weighing about 20% of her body, that is half a kilo. She watches the burrow while the male sits on the egg.

The small kiwi looks exactly like its parents except that it is a mini version, and it is brought up only by the father.

see also Kiwis; Lyre Birds

Flying Doctor Services

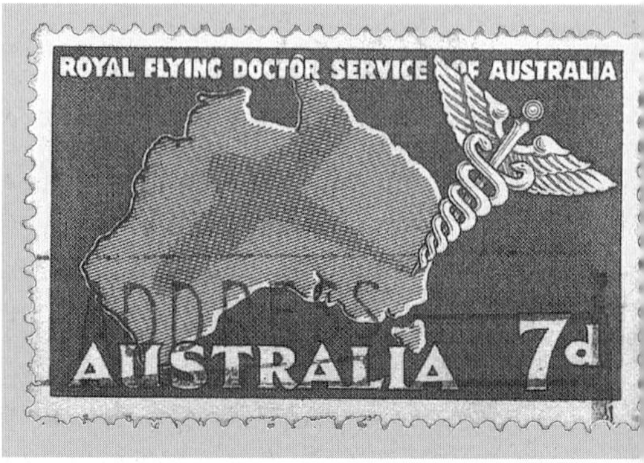

In 1912 the Australia Inland Mission was started by the Presbyterian church. This was the idea of John Flynn, a young minister. He saw the problems of Australians in the lightly populated central and northern areas of the continent. The Mission looked after some of the educational, social and medical needs of the people in the outback as well as the religious ones. The Flying Doctor Service was started by Flynn and the church for people living a long way from towns. It is well-known and an extremely important part of the outback services. When people first went to live in the outback, their contact with others was only by horse or camel. In emergencies they were alone.
The first problem was to find a way for each outback family to communicate immediately with others when help was necessary. It had to be a cheap and simple way as well. The answer made it possible to organise the Flying Doctor Service and was found by Alf Traeger, an amateur radio operator and electrical engineer. He designed a special radio. The operator sat on and pedalled a machine like a bicycle to make electrical power. This power went directly to the new specially designed two-way radio.
The operator could then send and receive messages. This new radio made great differences to the lonely outback life. People could talk to their 'neighbours' hundreds of miles away, giving information about floods, fires and other disasters and contact the doctor when necessary. When someone was ill, the doctor would talk to the people using the radio and tell them what to do and which medicine was needed. Each station had a special medical box.
However, at times the doctor needed to see the person immediately at their home or needed the hospital services. The radio system made it possible to discuss the problem, but there was no way of moving the patients to the hospital or for the doctor to make visits. The chance to buy a plane came in 1928. The Presbyterian Church and other voluntary organisations collected enough money. The doctor could now be flown to patients over a large area in the outback. There are fourteen bases in the outback today.

see also Outback Life

Food

Every country has famous and popular dishes that visitors may like or dislike. Here are some of the famous and important foods special to Australia.

Billy tea goes very well with a bush meal such as damper or bush bread. A "billy" is a bushman's kettle or saucepan, and is often an old tin with a piece of wire going across the top and tied on both sides for a handle. Two young branches with a fork, green so that they do not catch fire, are put on both sides of the fire and another strong green branch lies on the forks across the fire. The billy filled with water is hung on the cross stick over the fire to boil. When the billy boils, a handful of black tea and one or two gum or eucalyptus leaves are thrown in and the tea is left to draw. Before the tea is poured, the billy is swung. This is done in a clear place with a lot of space. The billy is taken in one hand and swung quickly in a circle parallel to the body several times. The centrifugal force keeps the boiling water in the billy and the heavier tea leaves are thrown to the outer edge of the circle, that is, the bottom of the billy. The tea, tasting slightly of eucalyptus, is ready for drinking.

Damper is well-known and well-liked by bushmen, men living in the country, and bushwalkers, people who walk and camp in the bush in their free time. When the campfire has burnt down and the coals are red and hot, flour, water and a little salt are mixed together. This is then baked in the fire. Sometimes it is put into a camp oven, two large metal bowls joined together, which is put in the hot coals to bake. The damper is best eaten fresh and tastes excellent when still warm. Other possibilities are damper twists, which sometimes have currants in the flour mixture. A handful of fresh dough is broken off and rolled into a long round rope. One end is put across the end of a green gum branch one to two centimetres thick.

The dough rope is then twisted round and round down the branch diagonally until it is completely covered for about ten centimetres. The branch is held over the coals and slowly turned until it is a golden brown. The damper twist is then carefully removed from the branch and filled with honey or jam and eaten hot.

Pavlova

is a famous and popular dessert eaten during the afternoon or as a dessert after lunch or a barbecue outside. Visitors also usually enjoy it. An Australian cook saw the Russian dancer, Pavlova, at the ballet. He found her dancing so beautiful that he made a new dessert, calling it after her. The almost white crust is fine and crisp, the inside soft, light and sweet. Traditionally the whipped cream on the top is covered with aromatic passion-fruit which are acid and make an tasty contrast to the sweet part.

Ingredients

4 egg whites
1 cup sugar (fine)
a pinch of salt
1 teaspoon vinegar
(or fresh lemon juice)
1 teaspoon vanilla essence

Put a pinch of salt and the egg whites in a bowl and beat until stiff and glassy. Gradually add the cup of sugar and beat well until it is dissolved. Add one teaspoon of vanilla essence and one of vinegar and beat in.
Now spread the mixture in a circle (about 18-20 cm in diameter and 4 cm high) on lightly oiled tinfoil or damp grease-proof paper on an oven tray. Bake in a slow oven (about 1 to 1.5 gas, 100°C electric) for one hour or until firm and crisp.

To serve

Turn the pavlova over onto a plate, so that the tinfoil is up. Remove tinfoil. Cover with 200-250 ml of whipped cream and top with passion-fruit (traditional) or red currants.

Notes:

- Fresh eggs are better.
- Moisture or egg yolk will stop the egg whites from beating.
- 2-3 packets of vanilla sugar can also be used instead of essence.
- The dark purple passion-fruit are the best.
- Any fruit can be used, but the ones listed are the best.

Peach Melba

is a dessert with ice-cream and fruit. It is named after Dame Nelly Melba, a famous Australian opera singer. Once when she was visiting Western Australia, a cook, also an Australian, wanted to make something new and exciting that she would enjoy eating.

Ingredients

3 large fresh peaches, white or yellow
fresh raspberries or raspberry syrup
sugar
vanilla ice-cream
whipped cream

Put 3 dessertspoons (2 teaspoons equal 1 dessertspoon) of sugar and about 2.5 cm of water into a saucepan and bring this to the boil. Add the peeled peaches carefully to the water, making sure they stay whole and cook them slowly. When cooked, remove them, cut into halves and put into individual dishes to cool. Wash the fresh raspberries and beat them into a sauce. Add sugar to taste.

To serve

Whip the cream until stiff. Place a scoop of ice-cream in the middle of each peach in the individual dishes. Put the whipped cream on top of the ice-cream. Pour the raspberry sauce or syrup over the top and around each peach.

Vegemite is something that is specially Australian and is found on most family and hotel breakfast tables. It is thick and dark brown and is put very thinly across buttered toast. It is a savoury spread made from yeast extract. Many Australians are addicted to it and once a strike on the vegemite production line continued so long that supplies ran out. The army is said to have gone to the unions asking them to let some vegemite be made as the soldiers were complaining about breakfast without it. A newcomer to an Australian breakfast table needs to know that vegemite should only be spread very thinly on toast, and not everyone likes it.

see also Eucalypts and Gum Tree;
Famous Australians; Outback Life

Glaciers (NZ)

The west coast of the South Island is famous for its ruggedness, beaches, fiords and glaciers. The rivers and glaciers have a lot of water as five metres of rain and snow fall in the area on average each year. The way to the glaciers is along the coast road. On one side is the ocean and sandy beaches or heavy surf and rocks. The surf is often high, rough and spectacular as it crashes onto the rocks and beaches. The ocean is the Tasman Sea, part of the Pacific Ocean and is a huge, wild piece of water where the southerly winds blow. These often bring cold air from the South Pole. On the other side of the road there are mountains rising up steeply and covered with thick native forest.

The Fox and the Franz Joseph Glaciers are both very unusual. This is because they both flow very steeply down the mountains and end so close to the sea although they are relatively near to the Equator.

No other glaciers in the world survive such "warm" temperatures so close to the sea. At the lower levels the glaciers flow through sub-tropical vegetation. There are several reasons why they flow so close to sea-level and do not melt although the temperatures are warm. Firstly, the places where their ice is made or their accumulation zones are very large because of the high snowfall. Secondly, they are very steep and the gravity makes them flow rapidly. Both the Fox and the Franz Joseph glaciers travel about a metre a day, over ten times faster than the Swiss glaciers. One example showing their speed is that some parts of a plane that crashed in 1943 took only six and a half years to travel the three and a half kilometres to the end of the glacier.

Living around the glaciers in the native forests are keas. These are greenish parrots, unusual because unlike the typical parrot, they love the cold and are not very brightly coloured. Their beaks are also very strong. They are not shy and notices warn visitors to be careful as the keas attack everything with their beaks in search of food. This includes car tyres and any soft rubber or cloth parts of cars and live sheep as it has been recently observed.

see also New Zealand – Areas and Regions

Glow-Worms (NZ)

On the edges of Lake Te Anau hidden below the forest floor are the Te Ana-au Caves which have whirlpools, waterfalls and a glow-worm grotto. Te Ana-au is the Maori name for "Cave of the Swirling Waters". The caves are mentioned in the Maori legends but were only re-discovered in 1948. A lot of work in the caves has made it possible to visit them safely and see the glow-worm grotto. The glow-worms are very sensitive insects and 'switch-off' their lights for up to two days if disturbed by any noise such as normal human voices.
The glow-worms in New Zealand are the larvae of certain insects called gnats. They produce the light chemically when they digest their food. The waste made as this happens has the quality of light. It is a brilliant blue, sometimes green.
The cave ceilings look like the sky on a dark, moonless night lit by thousands of tiny blue stars.
The adult gnats lay eggs on the cave ceiling. The larvae hatch from the eggs and stay stuck onto the ceiling for this part of their life cycle. They spin fine sticky webs which hang down into the cave, but cannot be seen by the human eye. Unlucky insects are caught on them, drawn up on the web string by the larvae and eaten. During this process the glow-worm glows.

see also Maoris; New Zealand – Areas and Regions

Great Barrier Reef

The Great Barrier Reef is in the ocean just off the coast of Queensland, in the north east of Australia. From its northern tip off the south coast of Papua New Guinea the Reef runs south for over 2,000 kilometres, becoming wider as it goes. This sheltered part of the ocean between the coast and the reef is over 200,000 square kilometres and there are about 700 islands in the area. It is the largest coral reef in the world. The ocean there is relatively shallow and a chain of coral reefs has grown up. The Great Barrier Reef has two main sections which are typical for coral reefs. In the inner part of the Reef, the coral, the numbers and colours of the fish and underwater plant life are not so spectacular as in the other section of the Barrier Reef, the outer reef. This is the wall of coral furthest from the coast which is still growing. This wall often catches the force of the waves coming from thousands of kilometres of open ocean to the east. The surf here is often continuous, rough and hard.

The islands are normally within the inner reef area and are of two types. The "low islands" are coral cays. These are made up of sand and dead coral pieces that have been blown there directly by the wind or carried there in the water flowing in the direction the wind comes from. As the wind slows down the sand and coral drop to the ocean floor and over the years build up to make an island. The coral cays are normally low and often have mangrove trees growing on the edge of the water. These are trees which grow in salty water and have special roots which grow up out of the water to collect air so that the tree can breathe.

Coral grows because polyps, small living animals, take calcium carbonate from the sea water and use it to make a protective coral structure around their bodies. There are about 350 species of corals on the reef which have many different colours. The colours come from the algae living in them. When the polyp colony dies, the algae also die and the sun slowly changes the coral to a white colour.

Recently, there have been two major problems facing the Great Barrier Reef. The sea star called the "crown of thorns" has increased in number. These feed on the polyps, killing them and therefore are a great danger for the continued life and growth of the Great Barrier Reef. Pollution of the sea water is the second problem. Water can be polluted by tourist development and mining for oil or of mineral sands.

see also Australia – Areas and Regions; Beaches; National Parks

Horse Racing (Aus & NZ)

Horse racing and going to the races is quite popular in **Australia**. In the early days of European settlement it was a good reason for people living in the bush to meet the neighbours and have fun in times when travel was not so easy. Horses were important from the time of the First Fleet for the new settlers to hunt for animals, for growing food and also for sport.
The military needed them for transporting men and goods. Most country towns have one or two annual race-meetings each year. The atmosphere at these meetings is very relaxed and friendly. They are often called "picnic races" and the whole family may go and take a picnic lunch. Normally a local ladies group will sell tea with sandwiches and cakes to make money for something, such as equipment for a kindergarten, youth club or senior citizens' club.
The most famous horse race in Australia is the **Melbourne Cup**. This is held on the first Tuesday of November, and this is always a public holiday in Victoria. Prizes for The Cup in 1996 were worth about $2,300,000 (Australian). Just over 90,000 people went to the The Cup in 1996. The race is now run over 3,200 metres, but was originally two miles and the best time was 3 minutes 16.3 seconds.
It has a large field, for example 22 horses raced in 1996. It is said that Australia stands still for this time. Once when international stock exchanges had a small crash there were no reactions on the Australian exchanges that day. It was Cup Day.
The atmosphere at Flemington on Cup Day is lively and varied. Some men wear formal clothes and top hats, and there is the "Fashion of the Fields" competition for the ladies. Others wear clothes of all sorts, and look like animals, Can-Can girls, Roman citizens and beer cans. There are also some very unusual hats, some are serious fashion with big feathers and others are for fun.
The fun hats are normally made at home and have anything and everything on them, such as toy horses racing around the edge in a mini Cup race. Most people wear casual dress and many go to relax and enjoy the day. The weather may be in the low 30s°C and sunny and dry or about 20°C and cold and rainy. Spring in Melbourne is variable. The Melbourne Cup has a long tradition and is the highlight of the spring racing carnival. Even people who do not normally bet often take a ticket in a Melbourne Cup sweep where each person in a group pays some money and has the name of a horse.
Whoever has the name of the first three horses receives some of the money.

Horse racing is also popular in **New Zealand**, especially in the South Island. One of the places which has regular race meetings is at Hokatika, the home of the Westland Racing Club. This is on the north-west coast of the South Island. Visitors watching the horses in the ring before the races can see the nearby mountains not far away which are snow-capped for many months of the year. The atmosphere is friendly and relaxed. For races over longer distances the horses start from an extension of the track which is within the car park. People standing near the finishing post to see the winners clearly when the race finishes can only see the jockeys and the horses' heads above the cars for about the first fifty metres of the race. Most of the track is surrounded by bush and forest. There is a local story about one of the **Jockey's Benefit Cup** races run many years ago. This is a race run to help jockeys who have not had a good season. It is said that for this race in that particular year all the jockeys riding in it sat down together and decided who should win. It was someone who had had bad luck all year and had not won a race. When the race started all was going to plan and the horses were running as they should have. However, as they came to the last few hundred metres, one of the horses which was not supposed to win started to run faster and the jockey could not hold him back. It looked as if he was going to win instead. Being a gentleman and wanting to keep the agreement as planned as that was the only fair thing to do, the jockey on the bolting horse fell off. Even if the horse had passed the winning post first, it would not have won. The right jockey is supposed to have won the race.

Hot Springs and Geysers (NZ)

Rotorua is in the centre of the North Island and the Maoris, the first New Zealanders, have lived there since the 14th century. The city is in the centre of an active volcano area. There have been many large eruptions or explosions from the volcanoes within the last hundred years. Together with the volcanic activity there are bubbling hot springs, boiling mud pools and geysers which shoot huge clouds of steam into the air. The largest and most interesting geysers, springs and mud pools are at the Whakarewarewa thermal park. Here, when the Price of Wales' Feathers geyser begins to blow clouds of steam that look like huge feathers, the Pohutu (Maori for 'big splash' or 'explosion') geyser next to it also comes into action. It sends up streams of hot water with huge white steam clouds between twenty and thirty metres high continuously for about twenty minutes at a time.
The eruptions happen because in the volcanic area the earth and rock just below the surface are hot and fluid. There is also water below the surface and this is heated as it touches the hot earth. The heat turns the water to steam. When the area below the earth is too small for the heated water and steam is pushed in all directions and escapes through a small open channel to the surface. The water from the geysers is usually a bright blue because of the minerals in it. There are four main colours around the geysers, the browns of the mud and minerals, the white of the steam, the bright blue of the pools of water from the geysers and the green of the plants that grow there. The whole area is humid like a sauna, smelling strongly of sulphur. The Whakarewarewa Park has native flowers, plants and trees of New Zealand. It is especially unusual because the streams flowing through it are hot and many pools of boiling mud are hidden amongst the bushes. Mud pools can appear overnight and if they throw mud up into the air it hangs on the bushes next to the living branches. The trees also grow around the pools of boiling water, but the steam prevents them from growing too close. Earlier the Maoris used the small boiling springs for cooking. The contrasts in the area are interesting, but it is dangerous to go too close to the geysers, pools and springs. A special path has been built so that visitors can walk safely through the park and also see everything.

see also Maoris

Immigration

The Kooris, the first Australian people have lived in Australia for more than 40,000 years. Since 1788, Australians of European background have lived there also. They either migrated or are descended from people who migrated. By 1868 no more convicts from British prisons were sent to Australia and all migrants were free settlers. For many, many years most migrants came from Britain, and this continued until after World War II.
In 1947 Australia had a population of 7.5 million in an area of 7,700,000 square kilometres. In this year the Australian Government decided the population had to grow. Since then there has been a large rise in the number of migrants and they come from many different countries. The decision to have more migrants and pay their fares to Australia was made after the Japanese bombed Darwin during World War II. It was clear that Australia needed a larger population for two reasons. One was to keep herself safe from other countries wanting to come and take her over to have more land. Therefore, more people were needed to fill her huge, empty areas. The other reason was, workers were needed to increase local production of goods and services. These workers also then had needs and made the local market bigger. At first the Australian Government tried to bring mainly British people to the country, but in the early 1950s they went to Holland, Italy and West Germany to find enough people. Refugees from Latavia, Estonia and Lithuania were accepted as migrants for political reasons. Yugoslavs also came and White Russians who had escaped to China after the Russian Revolution were allowed to come as well.
As conditions became economically better in Britain, less and less people were interested in migrating. The biggest change came when large numbers of Italians and Greeks

immigrated. These groups had fewer skilled workers and also did not usually have a knowledge of English. New arrivals settled in areas where relatives or friends lived and there are areas of Australian cities and suburbs which have a high number of Greeks or Italians. At one time Melbourne is said to have been the city with the largest Greek population after Athens. Both these national groups had a strong influence on certain aspects of Australian life. Two aspects are food and schools. The different types of fruit and especially vegetables that could be bought in the shops increased very quickly with, for example, zucchinis and garlic. Children attending school from the late 1950s were normally in a class with several different nationalities. During the period from the end of World War II to 1970, over three million migrants arrived in Australia. From 1976 on, about 25% of migrants to Australia have come from different parts of Asia. They have come for both political and economic reasons. Because of bad economic conditions in Australia such as unemployment, inflation and the loss of important markets because of the protectionist trade policy of the European Community, migration is much more limited today. People can only migrate legally for non-political reasons if there is a need for their skills. This change is important as it does not help anyone to come to a new country and then not find work. In general, however, many people who have had nowhere to go because of political changes have found a home in Australia from World War II up to today.

see also Convicts; Economic History; Famous and Influential People; Irish People; Kooris; Politics; Settlement of Australia

Irish People

Since the First Fleet arrived in 1788 there have been Irish people in Australia. Their influence shows in many areas and affected the development of Australia in her short history and can still be clearly seen today. Statistics show that there were about 70,000 Irish born people in Australia in 1981 when the last census was taken. A study on where the Australian population comes from showed that in 1978 about 2.5 million Australians out of a population of just under 15 million had Irish forebears. Irish influence shows itself clearly in the style and music of folksongs and in the Australian sense of humor. Some of the streets with the rows of two or three story houses or small factories found in the central areas of Cork, Dublin and Melbourne are so similar in style and atmosphere that it is difficult to decide which city they are in. The Irish have had a great influence on the development of Australia's education system, and the social and political situation.

The Australian Education System was based on "free compulsory and non-religious schools". The Irish Roman Catholic population wanted to have a religion as a part of school education. The result is that today all government schools which are the most usual, are non-religious, but both the protestant and catholic churches have primary and secondary schools. These church schools are called "public" or "private" schools and parents have to pay to send their children there.

The cost varies from school to school.

Most Australians would feel at home if they went for a beer at the local pub in Ireland or were invited to a meal with an Irish family.

see also Convicts; Immigration; Politics

Journeys Inland

The 7,700,000 square kilometres of the Australian continent and its coastline of over 36,000 kilometres meant huge areas had to be explored and mapped by the new settlers. The situation was difficult because of the dry climate, problems of permanent water, and a country so different from Britain. Just living from day to day was very difficult.

Unlocking the land behind Sydney was one of the difficult problems facing the new settlers in Australia. The first important and successful journey going inland and away from the settlements on the coast on the east of Australia was made by Blaxland, Wentworth and Lawson. This was so important because of the problems the new town of Sydney was having. By 1813 the population of Sydney had grown so big and there was not enough farming land. There was so little land because the Blue Mountains around Sydney made a wall and locked the city and the people into the small area on the coast. Many groups had tried to cross the mountains but they all had to turn back. The tops of valleys ended in steep cliffs of up to 200 metres high and it was not possible to climb up them. Blaxland, Wentworth and Lawson tried to cross the Blue Mountains in 1813 and succeeded. The forest or "bush" as the Australians called it, was thick and cutting a track was very difficult and slow. Often they could not travel more than one or two kilometres a day. They found the only small, narrow ridge that leads across the Blue Mountains to the wide open plains to the west. Today, a narrow winding road following this ridge is still the only way to cross them. Once this way was found, people could move out to start farms and build houses. More people could live in the area and food could be produced for them.

Crossing Australia from north to South was another difficult task. Many groups tried to cross the continent from north to south. Burke and Wills completed the first crossing from Melbourne in the south to the Gulf of Carpentaria on the north coast, a distance of several thousand kilometres. Because of bad luck, bad planning and Burke's inexperience and poor leadership, only one of the group lived to the end of the journey and told what had happened. Several of Burke's group died because they missed the group of people sent out to help them by only one day. The old eucalyptus tree with the message "dig here", cut into it to show the explorers where extra food was, can still be seen at Cooper's Creek.

The crossing of the continent from north to south was very important for Australia. The land was mapped and described and water supplies such as rivers, waterholes and springs were found. Much of the route explored by Burke and Wills was used for the Overland Telegraph Line which was finished in 1872. This was important for Australia as news could then be telegraphed directly to Britain and other countries and arrived very quickly. Up to that time news from Britain came by ship and at least six weeks were needed for the journey to Australia. A telegraph line could not be built before there were maps and information about the area Burke and Wills went through. Also the problems of taking a line through the desert areas of Australia and keeping it repaired had to be solved. Finding these answers was very important for Australia. The connection from the north coast to countries in South-East Asia was no problem. Many of these had governments from European countries or had large European-owned businesses and were already linked to Western Europe by telegraph. It was easy to extend south to the north coast of Australia, by laying an ocean cable. Burke and Wills' journey, although a disaster as most people died, meant that after Australia was soon linked directly by telegraph to the outside world the first time.

Crossing the Nullabor Desert from Adelaide to the West Coast was another big difficulty. The problems of water and a desert climate faced Edward Eyre on his journey of almost 1600 kilometres from 1839 to 1841. He began at Streaky Bay, west of Adelaide, and crossed the Nullabor Plain to finally arrive at Albany on the west coast. This trip is long and not without danger even today. Eyre was faced with an extreme situation. The Nullabor Plain's name comes from the latin words meaning 'no trees'. The scrub or low eucalypts which grow there are no more than two metres high if they reach this. Other areas are covered with tough native grasses like spinafix and grey-green salt bush, a plant that can grow in dry areas where there is a lot of salt. Only a few animals can live there. There is very little water. Wandering or moving sand dunes or hills, which move as the wind passes over them, cover everything in their path. This makes travel difficult and kills any plants that grow there. Eyre only finished the journey because the Kooris, the first Australians, had very good knowledge of the desert and knew how to travel through it. They helped him several times. Today, driving a car on the modern road it takes two days to cross the Nullabor Plain. This highway includes the longest stretch of straight road in the world.

Exploring the North-East of Australia

was taken on by Ludwig Leichhardt, born in Trebatsch near Berlin, Germany. He explored large areas of the Northern Territory. In 1844 he travelled 3200 kilometres from Brisbane to Port Essington near Darwin. He disappeared in 1846 while trying to cross the continent from east to west, and nothing of his party or goods have ever been found.

see also Australia – Areas and Regions; Camels; Economic History; Explorers; Settlement of Australia

Kauri Trees (NZ)

Mature kauris – Agathis australis – are huge, beautiful trees found in the North Island forests of New Zealand. The kauri is related to pine trees, but has long, thick, wide leaves which are often a little red in colour. Some kauris are as old as 1500 years and grow to 36 metres in height.
Interesting and unusual is that the trunks of the trees are up to three metres in diameter for the first thirty metres. In world standards, this makes them one of the trees with the largest amount of wood compared to height.
The wood is a deep orange-brown and excellent for furniture and boats. The Maoris used it for their highly decorated war canoes. The gum, taken from the trees by cutting a 'V'-shape into the bark, was used to produce an excellent wood varnish. "Gum diggers" also dug around the bottom of the trees looking for pieces of gum. The industry stopped when synthetic varnishes were developed. This was important for the kauri forests as the trees roots grow near the surface. The gum diggers often damaged the roots so much that the trees died. Taking gum constantly also finally killed the trees.
Of the original three million hectares of Kauri forest in the North Island, only about 10,000 are still there today. A lot of the forest has been taken for commercial use. Today this area is protected and new areas are being planted, but it takes many years and a lot of time looking after the trees when they are young before a new kauri forest does not have to be looked after.

see also New Zealand – Areas and Regions

Kiwis (NZ)

The New Zealand word "kiwi" has several different meanings. The flightless night bird is called "kiwi", and is a popular symbol in New Zealand. It is often printed on T-shirts. New Zealanders often call themselves "Kiwis" when asked their nationality. This is, of course, an informal answer. Apart from this, the word "kiwi" also means the kiwi fruit. This was first grown and developed as a fruit for commercial markets in New Zealand. It is exported to most countries throughout the world and looks a little like the brown body of the kiwi bird.

see also Flightless Birds

Kooris or Aborigines

The Kooris were the first people to come to live in Australia and were called "Aborigines" by the early European settlers. They have lived in Australia for more than 40,000 years. There are many islands from Australia to the Asian mainland to the north. Evidence shows that the Kooris arrived in Australia by travelling from island to island. The distances were never more than 75 kilometres and they travelled in canoes and small boats. The Kooris' culture was complex and rich. It included a meaningful and important religion as a part of daily living. In the social structure or the way people worked with each other and lived together, co-operation and sharing were important. There was a lot of free time to enjoy and excellent food including plenty of fruit, vegetables, meat and often fish.

The Kooris' life-style was designed around the climate – rainfall and temperature and seasonal changes -, the vegetation and soil, and bird and animal life. The natural environment stayed constant for thousands of years and the tribes lived well, although some years were better than others and hard times came with periods of drought. This is very different from the changes the European Australians have made to the environment since 1788. During the time when the Kooris were alone in Australia, they used a carefully designed system of burning off the grass and bush. They divided their lands into sections and burnt off a different area regularly. This cleared the land and let new, fresh grass grow. Forests did not grow in these areas. The grasslands where the plants grew that the kangaroos, emus and other animals ate were well kept. This was a good system as the animals could live and were an important food supply for the Kooris. The vegetation is special to Australia and did not die out because of the fire, but grew back strong and healthy.

Food depended on where the Kooris lived. Fishing was important for all Koori tribes who lived near the coastal and in the river areas. Tribes living on the rivers built very complex channels in the river beds for catching fish. Many different fruits, nuts, roots and plants were collected, including the grains of the grasses for flour. Some plants and roots were put in water for a time to remove poisons before cooking. Most food was cooked over the fire or baked in a hole in the ground as the Kooris had no waterproof containers. Both fishing and collecting plants were women's work. Hunting was done by the men. The tall and slender bodies of the Kooris is ideal for spear throwing but not for using arrows. Spears were important for hunting animals. A good hunter could hit an animal up to sixty metres away using a spear thrower.

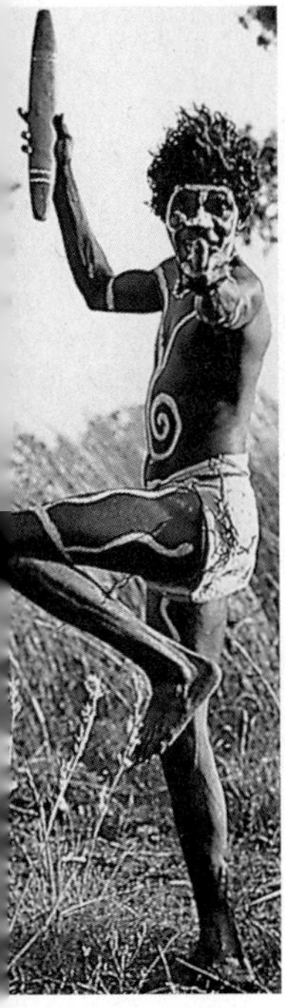

A spear thrower was a long piece of light wood curved up at the sides. A spear was laid across it and the thrower had this in his hand when he threw the spear. He was able to throw much further using this. During hunts the hunters communicated by a highly developed sign language as talking would have frightened the animals. Kooris were also highly skilled at following animals long after they were many kilometres away.

Tribes or groups of Kooris living together were between 500 and 1,500 in size. In areas with a lot of water and plants the tribes had more people. Control of the size was possible through special social rules. Important decisions for the tribe were made by fully initiated members. These men had many years of experience and the tribe saw them as wise and responsible. Contact with other tribes was through complex trade routes controlled by complex laws. Travel generally only took place within the context of these laws as help from the spirits was not possible outside tribal territory. Kooris were bound emotionally and spiritually to their land. Within the tribal territory there were sacred places. Kooris worshipped the ancestral spirits from whom they were directly descended. These were their own personal totems such as an animal, bird or tree. The dreamtime is their name for their religious beliefs. Clans or small groups with family members were sub-groups within the tribe. It was a very complex system with very strict rules about marriage, relationships and behaviour in all situations. Research shows that the rules and movements of chess are a child's game in comparison to knowing and organising the clan system.

see also Bunyips; Boomerangs; Dingoes; Dreamtime; Explorers; Famous and Influential People; Farming; Immigration; National Parks; Northern Territory; Politics; Settlement of Australia; Uluru and the Red Centre

Lightning Ridge and Opals

Lightning Ridge is about 800 kilometres north-west of Sydney in New South Wales. The town is in one of the most important opal producing areas in Australia. More than 90% of the opals in the world are found in Australia. Cooper Pedy and Andamooka are the two other important opal areas apart from Lightning Ridge.
There are three main kinds of opals. The **blue opals** are really a very fine layer of a white opal placed on a black background. This gives them the blue background colour. They are then covered with clear plastic. The firey colours of the rainbow show themselves against the blue background when the opal is held and moved in the light. The **white or milky opals** are solid stones of different sizes. They normally have either lines of blue and green or red, orange and yellow fire. The depth and amount of colour in the milky opals is intensive but changes with the light and the way the stone is held. The **black opals** are rare and the most valuable. These are also called fire opals because their colours are much deeper and stronger than all others. When the light hits them, the colours light up as if the stone is on fire. Most of the black opals are found at Lightning Ridge.
Opals were first discovered at the Ridge in the 1880s but it was not until early this century that they were mined commercially. The town was a real miner's camp until recently. It only had goods and services to cover the very basic needs of the miners. The buildings were often temporary, fairly roughly built and usually without air-conditioning although the temperature is often over 40°C. The town is now larger and has modern air-conditioned shops and motels. There is also a swimming-pool with water from an artesian bore, a race track and many other possibilities for free time. Today there are more and more tourists visiting the Ridge as well as people just trying their luck. In August there is an annual Opal Festival.

see also New South Wales

Lyre Birds and Other Rarities

There are about 700 kinds of birds native only to Australia compared to the 950 in Europe and Northern Asia together. Many Australian birds have beautiful colours and interesting, pretty or unusual songs and calls. The first sailors entering Swan River on the south-west coast of Australia could not believe their eyes when they saw birds the same as swans, but black ones, not white. Australian swans are black with a red beak. In the bush or forest today there are blue and red rosellas, yellow, green and red parrots and flocks of blue or yellow budgerigars that make clouds of colour when they fly. Galahs and cookatoos are also beautiful and brightly coloured in white and yellow, grey and pink, and black and red or yellow. They have a loud unmusical call.

The **lyre bird** with its grey, brown and white feathers is famous for his song. During the season when the male is looking for a female he builds a small hill or mound in a clear area in the bush. When his mate is near, he goes to his mound to attract her. He fans or spreads out his tail which looks like a lyre, a musical instrument. This is where the bird's name comes from. The lyre bird dances and sings with his lyre tail held high to make his new

mate happy. His singing is very pretty. His own call is followed by perfect imitations of other melodious birds living near him such as the whipbird, the bellbird and the laughing jackass, whose calls sound like their names. He also includes other sounds he has heard frequently. Previously, large trees needed for wood were cut by teams of two men. One stood on each side of the tree and held a long cutting saw, pulling and pushing to work the saw back and forth through the tree trunk. At this time two of these workers who were living alone in the bush thought someone was cutting a tree in their area. After listening and looking, they discovered it was a lyre bird imitating the noise their saw made while singing for his mate.
The **emu** is the second largest bird in the world. It is like the African ostrich which is the largest. Emus have a large body covered with brown and black feathers that "sits" on two long, thin legs. They live in groups. When they are frightened they walk with their black heads held high on, moving their long dark necks back and forward. If the danger is too high, they begin to run and can reach a speed of up to fifty kilometres an hour.

Emus live in the drier areas of Australia where large grassy plains are plentiful. Their nests are very rough but large enough to hold between five and twenty large blue-grey eggs. The female lays the eggs but then the male looks after the family, sitting on the eggs for about eight weeks without food or water. He then takes care of the young for six to eighteen months. The young emus are easy to see as they have wide stripes from head to tail of white and brown.

The **kookaburra** or **laughing jackass** is the largest kingfisher in the world although he does not often have the chance to catch fish. The early explorers were very angry because sometimes when they had problems a kookaburra would begin his call – pointing his beak to the sky, raising his tail and laughing long and loud. His call can really be best described as a laugh, and he has several different ones. Mornings and evenings the family group all join in to give their territorial call. This warns other birds not to come into their area. During the day they have other calls to find each other and in season the male has a mating call. Young kookaburras stay in the family group for up to four years before they leave to start a new family group, and pairs stay together for life. Kookaburras may live for twenty years or more. This is very important as each pair only has two or three young birds a season.

Kookaburras live in the bush where large eucalyptus trees grow.

They are well-liked and seen as friends as they eat snakes, even those more than a metre long. To catch snakes, the kookaburra sits on a branch and watches the grass below. If a snake comes it dives down, takes it in its large strong beak and flies back up to sit on the branch. To kill it, the kookaburra lets the snake fall to the ground and the snake's back breaks when it hits the earth. It also eats lizards, frogs, insects and other small birds.

see also Animals; Flightless Birds

Maoris (NZ)

The Maoris are the people who already lived in New Zealand when the Europeans arrived. The Maori legend tells that one of their heroes, Kupe, who was an excellent navigator, first visited "The Land of the Long White Cloud" in the 10th century. Over the centuries more people sailed to New Zealand from Polynesia to start a life in the new country. The moa, a huge flightless bird, was their main food. Today there are none living. The Maoris' culture is shown in complicated designs tattooed onto their bodies and cut into the wood of their houses and canoes.

By the late 18th century sealers and whalers were visiting New Zealand regularly. This was very bad for the Maoris. Firstly, they caught diseases from the Europeans. Illnesses that were mild for a European were serious for them. These were new and their bodies could not fight them easily. Many, many Maoris died. Secondly, the Maoris also traded jade for guns with the Europeans. Tribal wars started, and now they fought with guns and many people were killed. By 1830 the Maori population was falling rapidly. In the 1840s Samuel Marsden, the first missionary, organised medicine for them to help fight the European diseases. He also helped them to stop fighting and killing each other. However, the old traditions and ways of life had been changed for too long and the Maoris were not able to start living in the old ways again.

In 1840, the British sent Captain William Hobson to New Zealand. His job was to persuade the Maoris to become British citizens. A meeting took place at the Bay of Islands, on the east coast of the North Island. Forty-five chiefs agreed to sign the agreement and later five hundred chiefs signed. There was one big problem as the British paid very little for the land. The Maoris did not always want to sell and also needed land to live on themselves. The British took more land but only wanted to pay a low price for it. The Maoris did not want to sell. Hone Heke, the first chief to sign the original agreement, climbed the hill at Kororareka and cut down the British flagpole. The British put up a new flagpole and had more soldiers protect it, but the Maoris managed to chop it down four times. The British put a reward of £100 on Hone Hoke's head. In answer to this, Hone Heke offered £100 reward for the Governor's head. Hone Heke made his point and the British respected him more, but the final result was not clear. However, this event possibly influenced the British attitude towards the Maoris. It showed they were able to meet the British in the way they were used to. The Maoris were given the vote in 1867, showing that the British accepted them as equals.

Although the fighting was less after Hone Heke's actions, the Maori population continued to fall for some time. The Maoris also put a lot of energy into trying to keep what they still had of their culture and go back and try to find more of the old ways and have their old identity again.

Today the Maoris make up about 9% of the population or just over 300,000 people and are integrated into the society fairly well, while keeping their own identity.

see also Glow-worms; Hot Springs and Geysers; New Zealand – Areas and Regions; Pokutukawa Trees

Mount Egmont (NZ)

Mount Egmont is in the North Island of New Zealand. The mountain, known as "Taranaki" to the Maoris has special meanings for them. It had a very special religious meaning to them as a place for chiefs who had died and was also important as a place to hide in times of danger.
Mount Egmont or Taranaki is a 2,518 metre high volcano that is not active. It is about 3,000 years old. The last volcanic explosion was just before Captain Cook arrived. The mountain is well-known for rapid changes in temperature, falls of about 30°C have happened within 48 hours.
The rainfall on the west side of the mountain is almost 6 metres each year. The mountain has one of the most difficult areas to ski in New Zealand and an interesting 55 kilometre walking track around the whole mountain. The track is between 500 and 1,500 metres above sea-level.
It takes three or four days to walk the complete track because it is so rough. There are almost thirty river crossings with many waterfalls and gorges. Parts of the track include steep falls and climbs with ladders and rock steps. Views vary from the ocean to the west to the green inland with plains and hills to the east. There are a lot of different types of trees, plants and grasses. On the east side, thick forests of fifteen metre high kamahi trees with their twisted trunks and thick, dark green leaves make a strange atmosphere. Further on the track passes rock pools and Lake Dive, which is surrounded by the huge rounded lava forms. In other areas there are native trees with colours from green to blue and silver-grey. The open grass country is gold-brown and in summer clematis, a climbing plant with white flowers and rotia, a red wild flower both add colour.

see also New Zealand – Areas and Regions

National Parks

A national park is an area of land that is unusual and typical for a particular region. It has usually not been used for farming or building. The aims are to keep such areas as they are naturally, without man's influence, to save animals, birds and plants, protect the land in general, and give people a chance to see the land unchanged by people. Australia has over 13.5 thousand square kilometres of national parks, almost 4% of the country. Many more areas are expected to be named national parks in the future. Each state has many parks of all sizes and with many different kinds of land, plants and bird and animal life. Some parks include sacred places of the Kooris, the first Australians, which often have rock paintings.

New South Wales has more than fifty parks. **Kosciusko National Park** includes Mount Kosciusko, Australia's highest mountain and the "high country", flat and mountainous areas which often have snow in winter. **The Royal National Park** includes the coast with cliffs and beaches to the south of Sydney. Here there are steep valleys that have been cut by water through sandstone plateaus. These now have native eucalypt forests growing on them. Both the **Blue Mountains** and the **Karongra Boyd Parks** have rough valleys and cliffs. These areas have many trees, especially eucalypts. There are many beautiful views and waterfalls in both.

The Northern Territory has many world famous parks. **Uluru** is the Koori national park in Central Australia. The huge red monolith or round rock called **Uluru** or **Ayer's Rock** by many Europeans is there. The area is desert and the soil a deep orange red. There are many other parks in "The Territory". **Kakadu,** about 200 kilometres east of Darwin, is famous for its bird, animal and plant life. It is in the tropics and has a monsoonal climate of a wet and dry season. There are wide rivers and rich, green, tropical vegetation.

Queensland has more than two hundred and eighty national parks. **Daintree National Park** includes very important areas of tropical rainforest on the west coast north of Cairns. This is near the Great Barrier Reef, famous for its coral and colourful fish. Many of the Reef islands here are either completely or partly national parks. The Atherton Table area, west of Cairns, has many small parks which include spectacular limestone caves. There are also large parks in the drier areas of Queensland, such as the **Simpson Desert National Park**, where no-one lives.

South Australia has nine large parks. **Flinders Ranges** is in a semi-arid area and has the typical brown, red and orange earth and rocks found in the Centre. There are many gorges and dry river beds with a few waterholes. Huge river red gums grow here. Their wood is not destroyed in water. Many birds, especially brightly coloured parrots, and animals such as wallabies, kangaroos and emus live here.

Wilpena Pound, an oval-shaped hill with high grass and tree-covered walls rises out of the flat area around it. The Pound has no top like a normal hill but has a huge, flat hole in the middle which is a huge natural amphitheatre covered with grass and a few trees. Strong pinks, purples and blues usually colour the hills and land at dawn and dusk here.

Another park is **Coorong National Park**. This runs along the south coast in the east of the state and includes the mouth of the Murray River which rises near Mount Kosciusko in New South Wales. It has unusual beach and sand dune vegetation and is famous for the many varieties and large numbers of birds which live there.

Tasmania has over 14% of its area as National Parks. It is a very rugged island and generally has snow in winter. **The Cradle Mountain – Mount Saint Clair National Park** is the most famous. The direct walk of about 80 kilometres passes through a variety of country from moors to beech forest. The Australian natural beech has much smaller leaves than the European one. The southern area was covered with ice and glaciers in the Ice Age and there are many lakes and steep cliffs cut into the land the ice.

Victoria has more than twenty-five national parks. These include small ones such as the **Organ Pipes** west of Melbourne. The "Organ Pipes" are made of lava from a volcano. The lava stayed in the ground, cooled and became solid. A river washed the earth away and now these dark grey-black pipes make a cliff on one side of the river and look like organ pipes. Victoria also has beautiful areas of temperate rainforest with huge eucalypts, groups of acacia or wattle and huge tree ferns. Coastal areas such as **Wilson's Promontory** and the dry areas such as **Little Desert** in the north west of the state are other examples of the variety of the land. Western Australia has over fifty national parks. Some are famous for the colours, varieties and numbers of wild flowers that flower about September each year. In the **Stirling Ranges National Park** there are "black boys" which have a mass of fine, needle-like pointed leaves dropping out from the centre and a long spike with a flower coming up from the centre which turns black when the flower dies. The tall stem with the black heads are everywhere and give the plant its name. In the north there is the **Geike Gorge National Park** on the Fitzroy River in the Kimberleys. This has cliffs over a hundred metres high and is a gorge about ten kilometres long. The river has cut through an old coral reef. There are a lot of birds and animals in this park.

see also Animals; Australia – Areas and Regions; Eucalypts and Gum Trees; Great Barrier Reef; Kooris; New South Wales; Northern Territory; Queensland; South Australia; Tasmania; Uluru and the Red Centre; Victoria; West Australia

New South Wales

New South Wales (N.S.W.) is in the east of Australia and has nearly 2,000 kilometres of coast. N.S.W. is about 10 percent of the area of Australia. The southern border to Victoria is the Murray River. This flows down from the Great Dividing Range which runs along the east coast from north to south of the continent. The Snowy Mountains are part of this and Mount Kosciusko – 2,228 metres high – is found there and is the highest mountain in Australia. There is usually snow on it in winter. To the west of the mountains the country opens out and is mainly flat.
The Darling River runs through these and when heavy rains fall the whole area can be covered with water.
The rainfall in many western parts of the state is low. There are cattle and sheep here and wheat and other grains are grown. Several areas are irrigated and citrus and stone fruit grow well. There are also several areas with vineyards where red and white wines are produced.
Sydney is the capital city and is on a harbour with many small bays.
The Blue Mountains, part of the Great Dividing Range, are around Sydney. The mountains are called the "Blue Mountains" because the eucalyptus oils from the trees evaporate into the air in the heat and this gives them a blue colour.
The population of N.S.W. was about 6.2 million in 1996, about one third of Australia's population. Over half the people live in Sydney and suburbs, and another 10% live in Wollongong and Newcastle, two other main cities.

see also Australia – Areas and Regions; Australian Capital Territory; Economic History; Lightning Ridge; National Parks; Opera House

New Zealand – Area and Regions

New Zealand belongs to the Polynesian Island group in the Southwest Pacific Ocean. No point on the land is more than 130 kilometres from the coast and there are always mountains and hills to be seen. There are two large main islands, the North Island and the South Island. These are about 1,600 kilometres from north to south. There are also several smaller islands, such as Steward Island to the south of the South Island. New Zealand's total area is about 270,000 square kilometres. The North Island with just under 120,000 square kilometres is smaller than the South Island. This has about 150,000 square kilometres. New Zealand is in the huge Pacific Ocean. Part of this, the Tasman Sea, is on the west and separates it from Australia.
New Zealand's coastline is more than 5,000 kilometres long. There are beautiful long beaches, some with calm blue-green water and others with heavy white surf. There are also rocky beaches and cliffs, especially on the West Coast of the South Island. There are many bays and small islands everywhere, which makes it a wonderful place to sail. However, heavy storms and strong winds coming in from the Pacific make it dangerous for those who have not sailed often.
Lakes are found nearly everywhere in New Zealand. In the North Island these are often in the volcanic areas and water has filled old volcanoes. One example is Lake Taupo in the centre. This has an area of about 600 square kilometres and is the largest. The lakes in the South Island are mainly in glacial valleys in or near the Southern Alps. Most of the rivers in New Zealand flow very quickly. Some are good for white water canoeing, but not for general transport.
There are also hundreds of waterfalls throughout New Zealand. The fifth highest waterfall in the world is at Milford Sound in the South Island. It is called the Sutherland Falls and the water drops over a 500 metre cliff made by a glacier and into the fiord below.

The North Island

It is famous for its volcanoes, geysers and hot springs as well as for its beautiful beaches and bays. There are the following three main areas:

The Volcanic Region and the Western Hill Country

This is the central region of the North Island. There are many active volcanoes such as Mount Ruapehu and Mount Tongariro, although they have been still for a long time now. This volcanic activity is everywhere in New Zealand and there are about 400 earthquakes each year. Only about a quarter of these are strong enough to be felt. The worst earthquake recorded was in 1931 in the Hawke Bay area in the North Island. People died and the cities of Napier and Hastings were badly damaged. Today, some of the underground steam from the volcanic area is used for making electricity.

The Northern Peninsula and the Waikato Basin

This area covers most of the north of the island. There are flat, low areas and low hills. The forests are mainly evergreen trees and tree ferns which are typical in New Zealand. The few areas of the famous Kauri forests are here. The west coast has many long, sandy beaches, including one of a hundred kilometres. The east coast has many bays and an interesting coastline. The "Bay of Islands" is especially beautiful. Fingers of land reach into the sea and sailing and fishing here are excellent, especially as the water here is protected by land from the strong ocean winds.

The Eastern Hills

The east of the North Island has a low mountain range or chain of hills running down it, called the "Eastern Hills". The eastern side is mostly rugged. Some areas are national parks, but it is mainly used for sheep and cattle farming. The western side has more gentle hills and is better land. This is used for dairy cattle and lambs.

The South Island

The South Island has a generally colder climate than the North Island and the weather is more changeable. Visitors are told always to take an umbrella although the sun often shines. The West Coast has about seven metres of rain each year. The South Island, like the North, also has three main areas.

The Otago Plateau and Basin and the Canturbury Plains

The Otago Plateau and Basin are rolling hills and plains down in the south-east. The climate is generally cooler and wetter, and not many people live there. Sheep farming is the main activity. The Canturbury Plains are in the central east part of the island and surround Christchurch, the capital of the south. This is the largest flat area in New Zealand and usually green with the Southern Alps in the background. The plains are important for farming, especially for growing grains such as wheat and barley.

The Southern Alps and the High Country

This is the largest and most famous area, covering most of the South Island. Mount Cook or Aorangi which means "loud piercer", is the highest mountain. It was called this by the Maoris, the first New Zealanders, because it is so high and often pierces or cuts into the clouds. The first is the name used by the first European visitors to New Zealand. The whole of this area is very beautiful. There are still glaciers, rivers of ice, in the Southern Alps today. This is unusual as the climate is not as cold as in the European countries which have glaciers. Excellent skiing conditions are also found everywhere. Below the snowline are thick evergreen rainforests. All along the south-west coast there are long arms of deep water or fiords that cut into the land. It is possible to explore many of these by boat, but care must be taken because there is often bad weather.

see also Explorers; Glaciers; Hot Springs and Geysers; Kauri Trees; Maoris; Mt Egmont; Pohutukawa Trees; Sheep

Northern Territory

The Northern Territory or "The Territory", is in the centre of the northern area of Australia. It is a very big area of about 1.35 million square kilometres, with only 177,700 people living there. More than two thirds of these live in towns and nearly 30 percent are Kooris, the first Australians. The 6,200 kilometres of coast is mainly low and flat. There are many sandy beaches but also areas of mud with mangrove swamps. Mangroves are trees that grow in salt water at the edge of the sea and their roots are under water when this is high, and out of water when it is low.
There are two main seasons in the northern part of "The Territory". The "winter" is warm and dry, from about May to September. The "summer" is hot and wet. Some areas, for example Darwin, the capital city, have over 1,800 mm of rain a year mainly from November to March.
The heavy rainfall runs into many large rivers such as the Alligator and the Victoria, which cut their way through the land to the coast. There are many spectacular gorges and valleys cut into the red, brown and orange stone. Going south, the climate and land changes to become dry and hot. There are only low hills and flat country, including the Tanami Desert. The rivers there only run sometimes.
The best known part of "The Territory" is the south. This is called "The Centre" and has the Olgas, Ayer's Rock or Uluru, the Finke River with Palm Valley and the Macdonnell Ranges with many waterholes. Alice Springs, the main town in the area, has only 25 cm of rain on average each year and about 20,000 people live there. Altogether there are only three other towns with more than 3,000 people in "The Territory".
In general development in "The Territory" has been slow because of the climate and problems of water. The first important development was the Overland Telegraph from Adelaide to Darwin. This went across the continent from north to south through very dry desert areas, and was completed in 1872. It linked all major Australian cities and the whole country directly to the world for the first time. Until 1911, "The Territory" was controlled by South Australia which invested much more in the southern areas around Adelaide. Later, the cattle industry increased and Darwin was developed in the 1930s for defence reasons. Roads were built which meant there was a train from Adelaide to Alice Springs and then a highway to Darwin. This meant there was a good connection crossing the continent through the centre from south to north for the first time. During World War II, when the Japanese were fighting against Australia there was more development to try to protect the country. After the war, many minerals were discovered and mining has brought money and some jobs. "The Territory" has had full political control over its affairs since 1978. Tourism is also now important, as many visitors want to see "The Centre" and Kakadu National Park, a beautiful tropical forest with large areas of water and many different kinds of birds.

see also Australia – Areas and Regions; Kooris; National Parks; Todd River; Uluru and the Red Centre

Opera House

One of the most famous buildings in Australia is the Sydney Opera House. It is on Bennelong Point where the First Fleet arrived in 1788. The white sails of the building stand out against the sky and the blue of the Harbour's water. Its design and the engineering techniques used while building it are very special in the world. There were many problems during the building period. The architect, Joern Utzon, who won the competition for designing the building had never been to Australia. He used photos of Sydney Harbour to draw his design. When building began, however, it was soon clear that the way the shells or sails could be built had to be changed. Building began in 1959 and was not finished until 1967.
The original expected costs of $7 million rose to be over $100 million. Most of this extra money was raised by the Opera House Lottery. Today, many cultural activities are held there and many people visit the building out of interest.

Outback Life

The "outback" is the Australian word for areas of bush and land a long way from large towns and cities. Some areas of outback are cattle or sheep stations, others are natural bush. The word "outback" also paints the picture of very large, open areas and freedom to move across fairly flat country that is often dry and dusty. Eucalypts, wattles and other native trees and plants grow there, but because the areas are often dry these do not grow very high and are often silvery-grey green in colour as protection from the sun. People who live in the outback today have the possibilities of modern equipment such as air-conditioning and travel either using four-wheel drive cars and trucks or most stations have at least one light plane. Two-way radio and the telephone make communication possible and easy. For general news and entertainment radio and television can be much more easily received since satellites can be used to receive these. Stations often have their own vegetable gardens and beef, lamb and possibly kangaroo meat are often served at meal times. Artesian water helps during the dry periods, especially if it does not have too many minerals in it. The day usually starts early for those in the outback because of the heat. It is not unusual to get up at 4.30 am and be working by 6.30 am. Younger children who have their lessons with "The School of the Air", a two-way radio system of teaching, may also have someone who helps them with their lessons and looks after them in general. Nearly everyone has a long rest in the afternoons because the heat makes it impossible to work. Jackaroos are station workers whose main jobs are to look after the sheep or cattle in the huge paddocks of many square kilometres. They keep the fences in good order so the animals stay where they should be. This is very important as these are often left alone for long periods. The area is so huge that if they get out it is very difficult and takes a lot of time to find them again. Jackaroos may spend weeks away from the station, working alone and camping out under the stars. A Jillaroo is a young woman doing the same job.

Outback towns are very different from those in areas with more people. One example is Meekatharra, a town of several hundred people in the north-west of Western Australia. The main street is a wide, dirt or earth road which is very dusty. The town has pubs, a general store, a restaurant serving mainly steaks as fresh vegetables are not easily available, an outdoor cinema (as it hardly ever rains). It also supplies other basic needs such as petrol and services needed by those in the area. Meekatharra serves the people in a very large area. Perth is about 650 kilometres to the south, Port Hedland 700 kilometres to the north and Carnavon is 500 kilometres to the north-west. To the east is the desert. Other settlements or towns in the area have petrol station and probably a pub, but not much more.

see also Artesian Water; Australia – Areas and Regions; Bushfires; Camels; Cattlemen in Choppers; Flying Doctor Service; Food; Pubs; School of the Air; Sheep; Waltzing matilda

Pohutukawa Trees (NZ)

The flowers of the pohutukawa tree are groups of red spikes or stamens and the trees are a mass of colour in December, for Christmas. These huge, wide trees grow around the northern beaches of the North Island and have important spiritual meaning to the Maoris, the first New Zealanders. One tree is the last place for the spirits of this world to move into the next. The flowers are liked very much by birds because of their nectar, and the trees make shade which protects other plants. Beach erosion or the washing away of the sand and beaches is stopped when these trees grow because their root systems is wide and holds the sand in place. They also grow across and around rocks and hold these in place.
The pohutukawa is a hard wood tree and often lives for 200 to 300 years. Today there are certain problems facing the pohutukawas. After the land was cleared for farming, the trees did not re-grow. The seeds do not live through fire and so new trees do not grow amongst grass. A new tree also needs to be watered and protected for five years before it can survive alone. Another problem is the possum, a small climbing animal introduced from Australia in the 1800s. They eat a lot of the new young leaves. Farm animals also damage the roots as they eat the grass and plants below the trees.
To protect the tree and the coastlines, an organisation called "Project Crimson" as crimson is the bright red of the flowers, has been set up. Holiday makers are being told about the problems and how important the trees are. This includes the fact that even a small fire lit beneath a pohutukawa can kill it. Farmers are being asked to fence the trees in, and many new trees are being planted.

see also Maoris; New Zealand – Areas and Regions

Politics

The Australian Political System

Both federal and state political systems are similar. They each have a Lower and an Upper House, but Queensland has only the Lower House. The House of Representatives or Lower House has about 148 members who are elected for a maximum of three years.
The members of the Senate or Upper House, about 64, are elected for six years. Senators represent states as a whole. The members of the House of Representatives are different and represent one area within a state. There are about 70,000 voters in each electorate. A political party needs to have a majority of seats in both houses to govern. If no party has a complete majority, coalitions are made of two or more parties and possibly independents, members of parliament who do not belong to a party.

Voting starts at eighteen It is compulsory for everyone to vote in all elections. Only the Aborigines may choose, but if they register they must also vote. At state and federal elections in Australia the preferential voting system is used. In this system voters must put a number in the box next to every name. If they do not do this their vote will not be counted. This system gives the voters a chance to decide themselves who they think is the best person, and not to rely on a political party to do this for them. If their first choice does not win, their second, third and other choices count until someone has one more than half the total votes. In the example below, Quince cannot win as he has so few first votes. The vote counters take the voting papers again and look at the second choice. They now give these second choice votes to the other two candidates.

Ballot Paper

_____ Brown

_____ Peters

_____ Quince

First Count

Brown 2,982

Peters 2,708

Quince 1,010

Second Count

Brown + 756

Peters + 254

Political Parties

There are two main political parties in Australia – *The Liberal Party of Australia* and *The Australian Labor Party*. There are two other important parties. *The National Party of Australia* represents many farmers and usually forms a coalition with the Liberals. *The Australian Democratic Party* is the other and has held the balance of power in the Senate for many years. Neither of the larger parties had a majority in the Senate, and the Democrats had enough votes to make a majority. They vote on each issue as they feel right, and not always with the same party. As decisions are only made when both the lower and the upper houses agree, the Democrats help make decisions although they are only a small party. There are other small parties which win very few, if any seats, and several independent members of parliament.

The Power Balance between the States and the Commonwealth

The federal government began in 1901, but the states kept most of their powers. The power moved to the federal government because of the two world wars. It was necessary to co-ordinate all aspects of the wars and the economy of the country. This had to happen at the federal level. The key was finance, taxes and money. Today, the Federal Government gives the states about half of the money they need to run and build everything. The federal government looks after external affairs, foreign trade, immigration, the national finances, social services, communication and defence. Health, law and order, agriculture, energy services and education are shared with the states. The states concentrate on local issues such as education, housing, trade, the police and industry.

General Information

1856	•	manhood suffrage, that is, the right to vote in elections in South Australia
1859	•	use of the secret ballot for voting
1900	•	manhood suffrage in all Lower House elections
1903	•	introduction of old age and invalid pensions
1908	•	female suffrage in all Lower House elections

Australian Attitudes to Politics

Curse the Government and say the country's done. It doesn't matter what Government it is, for he's always against it. I never knew a real Australian who wasn't.

Henry Lawson (poet) 1900

Whoever you vote for, a politician gets in

Election Poster 1963

This is our first and greatest sin: we do not care. Preferring to regard politics as a 'dirty game' which we shall leave to others, . . . 'We have allowed too many of our political leaders to be men who are not worthy to hold such office'.

Edward St John, QC and former MC-1969

see also Australian Capital Territory; Education; Famous Australians; Immigration; Irish in Australia; Southern Cross

Pubs (Aus & NZ)

A pub is the Australian word for hotel and comes from the old name "public house". Pubs are found everywhere – in cities, towns and in the bush or country. An Australian country town normally has at least one pub. There is, as well, a general store, a petrol station, a sports oval, tennis courts, a place to play golf, a church and maybe a police station. But the pub is very important. As it is often a two-storey building and the ground floor is normally cooler in summer, the public bar and ladies lounge, a room with comfortable chairs and a quiet atmosphere, are usually found here. Even Williams Creek in South Australia with a population of four-teen has a pub. During the times of early settlement in Australia the pub was often used as the public hall for Saturday night dances, on Sundays the bar was a pulpit for the preacher leading the church service, and sometimes it was also used as a court room.
Pubs normally offer rooms to visitors wanting to stay overnight. From very early on, meals and rooms had to be part of the hotel service if the hotel wanted a license to sell alcohol. Travellers needed a place to eat and rest over night, not just to drink.

Very often other businesses grew up around the pub, starting a small settlement. In those times it was usually men who were moving around to open up the new country. The hot dry climate made life hard and the men in the pub were often out on their own. From this the tradition which became an unwritten law grew up – no women in the bar. Women took drinks in the lounge. Men could only enter the ladies lounge with a lady. This tradition was only completely broken when the Equal Opportunity Law was passed in 1977.
Today in real local pubs, the weather – drought, rain, floods, bushfires, sport and politics "Australian style" are often discussed. "Counter meals" are popular. Typical is grilled meat – huge steaks or lamb chops with vegetables or salad. People who have stayed overnight can enjoy a good breakfast. After cereal and orange juice comes the question,
"Owmanyeggswithyasteag, ndyawannudwelldun, medyum er rare?"
("How many eggs with your steak and do you want it well-done, medium or rare?")
Pubs in New Zealand also are places where people meet to talk and maybe eat a counter meal. They are found in every large and small town. They also have strict times for closing, usually 10 pm. Unknowing visitors may ignore the little bell that the barman rings at 9.55 pm. The locals know that that is the last chance to get a drink, alcoholic or non-alcoholic, for the evening. The visitor who asks for a drink after 10.00 pm will be disappointed, but is sure to listen to the bell the next time.

see also Outback Life; XXXX – Queensland's Beer

Queensland

Queensland is in the north-east of Australia and is almost 1.3 millions square kilometres, with a very long coastline of 7,400 kilometres. More than half of Queensland is tropical – it lies north of the Tropic of Capricorn towards the equator and has dry and wet seasons. The climate changes to be semi-arid in the central west and to arid in the desert areas in the south west. October to March is the hottest time, and temperatures are often over 40°C in the inland areas, but it is a dry heat. Mild winter temperatures and generally clear skies with a lot of sun make Queensland very popular for holidays. The coast areas and beaches with surf and clear blue water are excellent for swimming and diving. Many areas are developed, but it is still easy to find beaches where it is possible to be alone. There are very many large areas of natural bush and wilderness found only in the state and the Great Barrier Reef is off the north coast.

There are about 3.6 million people living in Queensland. About 40% live in and around Brisbane, the capital city. Most people live on the east coast, especially the south-east. Of the ten cities with more than 20,000 people, only two are not in the coastal area. Mt Isa is one, and it is a mining centre.

Development of Queensland first began in 1824 when the Brisbane River was discovered and a small settlement was built for convicts, the prisoners sent to Australia from Britain. By 1840 there were no more convicts and free settlers arrived. Growth was slow and by 1859 when Queensland was given political independence there were only 23,500 people living in the state. Cattle and sheep were the most important industries. Gold is still mined and sugar is still grown as in the early days. Wheat is also now important. Industry was slow to develop because of the low population and distance from other states and their markets. The biggest change came in the 1960s with mining. Minerals such as silver, zinc, bauxite and coal are found in Queensland, and today there is an aluminum plant at Gladstone.

see also Australia – Areas and Regions; Convicts; Economic History; Great Barrier Reef; National Parks; Politics; Sheep; Waltzing Matilda; XXXX – Queensland's Beer

Quokkas, Wallabies and Kangaroos

All these animals are related and many people call them all kangaroos. They are marsupials, that is warm-blooded animals with a pouch for carrying their young and are plant-eating animals. Their back legs are highly developed for jumping. A strong tail helps them balance when they travel quickly or slowly and when they sit.

Quokkas

Quokkas like to live in places which are very wet or swampy. They used to live in the south-west of Australia, but very few live there now. There are many quokkas on Rottnest Island near Perth, West Australia. The climate on the island is drier than in the south west. The Dutch explorer who discovered the island thought the quokkas were rats. The quokka, a relative of wallabies, is about the size of a cat. It normally grows to about 80 cm in length including its 30 cm long tail. This tail is very short compared to most members of this family. It is grey-brown or grey and has short round ears.

Wallabies

Some wallabies are smaller versions of kangaroos. The largest have a head and body length of about 1.3 metres and live in forests. Others include the smaller sandy wallaby, the black striped wallaby and the red neck wallaby.

Kangaroos

The giant red or plains kangaroo is the largest marsupial – the tail up to 100 cm and the head and body up to 140 cm long. They enjoy company, living in mobs or groups of up to a hundred on the open grasslands of the arid and semi-arid areas. They can be best seen at dusk or dawn when they feed. If the mob feels danger is coming, all the kangaroos take flight, jumping up and down smoothly in long regular jumps like gentle waves flowing across an inland sea. There are many kinds of kangaroos, some like open bushland

and others such as the eastern wallaroo are at home in rocky areas. The smallest kangaroo is the small dark grey-brown potoroo from 23 cm and 41 cm which likes to live alone. These can normally only be seen at night as they are nocturnal. They eat roots that they dig out of the ground and live in the thick grasses in forests with high rainfall.

see also Animals

Rabbits

The European rabbit is the worst animal pest in Australia. Some were brought with the First Fleet, but Thomas Austin, owner of a large farm near Geelong, west of Melbourne, is held to be responsible for the main problem. He imported twenty-four wild rabbits from England in 1859, and let them free so that he and his friends would have animals to shoot. Rabbits finally moved so far that they lived throughout Australia, even crossing the desert area of the Nullabor Plain to enter Western Australia.
There are two main problems. Firstly, the rabbits eat only certain plants which are very valuable and necessary for good and varied plant life. When these disappear, plants of little value often grow. Rabbits also eat the plants down very low, preventing re-growth. This is not the case with the native animals such as the kangaroo. Young forests are also eaten by rabbits, and so the new growth of trees to replace older, dying ones does not take place. Rabbits naturally compete with small native animals. Seven rabbits are estimated to eat about as much as one sheep. The second aspect which has made rabbits become a pest in Australia is their breeding habits. There are about six young in each rabbit family and rabbits breed between four and six times each year, if the conditions are good. In the cooler areas of Victoria and New South Wales rabbits breed only about twice but still have four to five young. As there are no natural enemies of the rabbit in the Australian bush, they increase rapidly.
Trapping, shooting and poisoning have been tried to control the rabbits. At one time they reached plague numbers and moved across the whole continent. The damage they did then to the natural vegetation was so great that even today some areas have not recovered.
It was so important and necessary to stop the rabbits, that rabbit-proof fences were built. These were not successful. The next important control tried was a virus called Myxomatosis, deadly to rabbits but not dangerous to man. Mosquitoes carrying it were let free. When they bit the rabbits they became ill and died. This controlled the rabbit population for a limited time, but now this no longer works. In 1996 the calisivirus was released as another attempt at control. However, the farmers and the people in the bush still try to control them by the old methods.

see also Animals; Farming

Rain-Making

Many areas of Australia are semi-desert or desert and cannot be used for farming or to support people. Many areas often have months without rain. Therefore the idea of man controlling and making more rain fall is interesting and would be valuable. There have been many studies and programs on rain-making in Australia.

The government-supported body, the Commonwealth Scientific and Industrial Research Organisation (CSIRO) started rain-making experiments just after World War II.

CSIRO studied the ways tiny water droplets in clouds came together to form water drops which then fell as rain. Small particles of dry ice or silver iodide dropped into a cloud from a plane 'seed' the cloud and rain may fall. All clouds are not suitable for seeding, however.

Rain-making is also difficult as rainfall varies from year to year in each area and, therefore, there is no constant pattern that can be used to measure any increase in rain coming from cloud seeding.

see also Australia – Areas and Regions

School of the Air

The "School of the Air" is part of the education system of Australia. It is a special program for children living in the outback areas a long way from other settlements. These areas in Western Australia, western New South Wales, Queensland, Northern Territory and South Australia have huge cattle and sheep stations of hundreds of square kilometres. There are very few people living in the areas and distances are huge. Naturally the children living in the outback cannot attend school unless they go to live in a boarding school during term. For these children on outback stations there are special correspondence courses for primary school. This is from the first school class up to year six. To support this, the "School of the Air" has been organised. Alice Springs in Central Australia is an important and well-known centre of the "School of the Air". Two teachers work here to teach children in the outback areas around Alice. Each day every grade has a special broadcasting time with a teacher when all children in that grade listen to the two-way radio to discuss the day's work, have play readings and share in an exchange of ideas and other information.

In the 1920s and 1930s when the pedal radio was used and planes were not common, this was a very important link for education. Today the "School of the Air" is the important daily link for children learning alone, but the teachers also travel around to the stations to meet and get to know the pupils. Also, meetings of class members are organised using the light planes which most stations have today for travelling.

see also Outback Life

Settlement of Australia

The First Human Settlement and European Discoveries

The history of human settlement in Australia is estimated to have begun more than 40,000 years ago. The first people are believed to have walked via the land bridges joining Australia to New Guinea. Others probably came by some kind of boat. European discovery was very late. There are indications but no definite evidence that Portuguese sailing-ships that had lost course saw land and possibly landed on the coast. Many ships lost their way because of the Roaring Forties, the prevailing Westerly Winds in the southern hemisphere.

Interest in the area increased when the Dutch came to the East Indies and began looking for new trade possibilities. Dirk Hartog, Captain of a Dutch sailing-ship, left a pewter plate with writing on it on the most westerly island of Australia in 1616. His countryman, Abel Tasman, was sent some years later to explore the area. He discovered Tasmania and mapped the north coast of "New Holland". As he found no trade possibilities and the land appeared too dry to settle, the Dutch ignored the country.

British Discovery and the First Fleet

In 1770, Captain James Cook discovered and named all the east coast for Britain. This coast and its hinterland contain the most fertile land of the continent. European or British settlement began here and today most of the population is concentrated in these areas.
The land looked and was fertile. However, settlement was slow because of two reasons. The first was the distance of Australia from the rest of the world. The second was that there were no goods which were valuable and easy to find or harvest, in contrast to the spices of the South-East Asian countries. Trading possibilities did also not exist.
The change and interest in settling Australia came after the American War of Independence against Britain. America naturally stopped taking British prisoners. As there were not enough prisons to keep all the prisoners locked up, the British had to look for an alternative. The decision was made to establish a convict or prison settlement in Australia.

see also Australia – Areas and Regions; Convicts; Explorers; Immigration; Journeys Inland; Kooris

Sheep (Aus & NZ)

In both New Zealand and Australia, sheep farming is important, although synthetic fibres have taken part of the traditional market. Much of the wool produced is exported. Often the female sheep are bred for wool, but paired with a meat-producing male sheep, so that the lambs can be sold for meat for the local and export markets.
The first step is to pair the sheep for lambing and control is kept so that infertile sheep can be found and sold. Soon after the lambs are born they have to have their tails cut off. Cutting off the tails is necessary to prevent infection in the hot weather. This rounding up of the sheep and lambs is often used as a chance to give medicine for protection against various diseases. Depending on the weather, the sheep may also have to be dipped to clean the wool or protect them from insects.
This is especially important in hot, wet weather.
Shearing is done each year, and in the woolshed there are shearers, wool sorters who sort the wool according to quality, and rouseabouts who do all the extra jobs such as seeing that the shearers have sheep, pressing the wool and cleaning up generally.
A good shearer shears between 200 and 400 sheep daily, varying with the kind of wool and the size.
All these jobs involve moving and separating the sheep in large and small areas. These jobs are possible because the farmers have highly skilled sheep dogs although many farmers today use motor bikes as well for the paddock work. The Australian kelpie, an excellent sheep dog, knows instinctively how to work with sheep but needs to be trained to obey commands as the farmer knows where he wants the sheep. A well-trained dog can be commanded to go into a huge paddock, group the sheep or "round 'em up", then "push 'em up" through the gates and along tracks to the yards and sheds.
Some dogs are natural "yard" dogs, jumping over fences and onto the backs of groups of sheep in the pens, barking or "speaking up" to move them. The kelpies snap at the sheeps' feet to make them move, but do not break the skin.
In Australia, sheep farm sizes vary from a 100 hectares in a fertile region to 10,000 square kilometres in the drier inland. The wool is used for many purposes, the Australian merino providing excellent wool for clothing, while the coarser New Zealand wool is well-suited for carpet and heavier clothing.

see also Cattlemen in Choppers; Economic History of Australia; Farming; Outback Life

South Australia

South Australia is in the centre of the southern part of Australia and is almost one million square kilometres in size. Its 3,700 kilometres long coastline is part of the Great Australian Bight. This is a rugged and spectacular coastline with sandstone cliffs dropping directly into the Southern Ocean. The ocean is a deep blue and heavy surf breaks on the cliffs. There are also white, sandy beaches stretching for kilometres.
Two bays, Spencer Gulf and St Vincent Gulf, cut deeply into the central coast. Adelaide, the state capital, is on the second Gulf. To the east is the Coorong coast which joins Victoria. This is sandy and has rolling dunes covered with grasses.
The Murray River starts in New South Wales to the east and reaches the sea at the Coorong coast, where there is a large national park especially known for sea-birds.
The western part of the state is low and flat. It is part of the Nullabor Plain. "Nullabor" means no trees and there are mainly grasses, bushes and low trees with many thin trunks. The Nullabor runs west through West Australia almost to the coast, and is a desert area. The Great Victoria Desert is in the north-west part of South Australia. Over 80 percent of the state has less than 250 ml of rain each year. There are many salt lakes there, for example, Lake Eyre.
This sometimes receives water from several rivers which only run when it rains. This may happen once every few years or, in a bad drought, only once every seven or more years.
The hard salt surface of Lake Eyre has been used by racing car drivers trying to break the world speed record.
North of Adelaide is the Barossa Valley, famous for its wines. Many German settlers went to live there late last century, and old graveyards often have stones with writing in German using Gothic writing.
The Flinders Ranges are further north in a semi-arid area. The desert wild flowers grow thickly and are like a colourful carpet in spring. The typical Australian desert colours of red, brown and orange are here in the Flinders Ranges. In the early morning and late evening the hills change colour and are pinks, blues and purples. There are many animals such as the large red kangaroos of the plains, smaller wallabies and emus. Cookatoos, black with red or yellow, blue and green grass parrots and yellow, green or blue budgerigars live around the waterholes.
The south-east part of the state including Adelaide has a Mediterranean-type climate.
The summer is hot and dry and the winters are cool and wet. Swimming and surfing are popular with people living near the coast, and the sandy beaches and blue water are very inviting. This is also the area receiving the most rainfall, about 750 ml each year. Almost 70% of the population of 1.48 million live in this area.

see also Australia – Areas and Regions; Beaches; Economic History; Explorers; Journeys Inland; National Parks

Southern Cross (Aus & NZ)

The stars in the Southern Hemisphere are very bright and many more in number than in the Northern Hemisphere. The Milky Way, a wide band of thousands of stars that give the sky a milky colour, runs in a wide path right across the night sky from one side of the horizon to the other. In this path lies the Southern Cross, a constellation of stars very special to Australia. It can also naturally be seen in the night sky above New Zealand. Looking at the sky on a clear night without a telescope, the Cross consists of four stars marking the tips of its two axes and an extra, small star between the lower righthand points. Two stars in a line point to the Cross and are called the "Pointers". The brighter of these two is really a group of three stars very close together. One is the closest star to the sun and the earth, and it is only four light-years away. There is no star marking south as the Northern Star in the northern sky. However, if the line of the long axis of the Cross is continued to the bright star Achernar, and half way along this a line is dropped at right angles to the horizon, south can be found.

Although many visitors to Australia are surprised that the Southern Cross is not a larger constellation of stars, its importance to Australians and their feelings for it show in many areas. The Cross is on the current Australian flag and that of New Zealand. In 1854 a dark blue flag with the Cross in white was the symbol of Eureka Stockade and the fight for rights. This was the only place and time in Australian history where citizens fought in an organised way with guns against the police. The problem began when the government introduced a licence fee for gold diggers that was so high that many could not pay it. The problem came to a head in Victoria, at Eureka, a part of the new city of Ballarat on an important gold field. Changes in the costs of the licence and also the right for every man to vote soon followed. Eureka is therefore seen as an important event in Australian history and is symbolised by the Southern Cross. Also many Australian folk-songs and poems mention the Southern Cross.

see also Southern Lights

Southern Lights (Aus & NZ)

The Southern Lights or "Aurora Australis" can be seen in the southern parts of Australia and the South Island of New Zealand. Aurora was the old Roman goddess of the dawn. Both the Southern and Northern Lights are caused by magnetic storms on the sun's surface. These storms send out magnetic waves which affect the earth's magnetic field by making it longer like a rubber band. The field comes closer to the earth at the Equator and is moved away from the poles to form an egg shape. When the storm finishes, the magnetic field changes back to its normal shape.

This activity makes strips and areas of whites, creams, reds and greens in the sky.

When the Southern Lights are strong, they can be seen all over Tasmania, in the southern parts of Victoria and New Zealand's South Island.

On a clear night huge areas of red crossed with stripes of white and green moving back and forward are seen. The complete southern part of the sky is a moving body of colour. The light is stronger than that of the lights of a large city viewed from a high hill nearby.

see also Southern Cross

Tasmania

Tasmania is sometimes called "The Apple Isle", as the climate is much cooler and milder than the rest of Australia, and excellent apples are grown there. The difference in climate is because Tasmania is the most southern state of Australia and, therefore, furthest from the Equator, and it is an island. It is separated from the mainland by Bass Strait, a narrow shallow channel of water that is very dangerous when there are storms. It is about 68,000 square kilometres in area, about 300 kilometres from north to south and east to west. This makes it the smallest state. There is thick rain forest on the west coast, and this area is still an area not farmed by man. There are many fast rivers where people now raft although it is very dangerous and a trip takes many days. Walking in the area is also popular, but there is more than 2,000 ml of rain each year.
The mountains here are steep and rugged and there are many lakes. The landscape was partly made by glaciers.
The central area has less rain because the "Roaring Forties", the westerly winds coming across thousands of kilometres of open ocean, leave much of their water on the west coast.
In the centre there is a very famous walking track of about 90 kilometres, the Cradle Mountain-Lake St Clair track. Native Australian beech trees with leaves much smaller than the European beech grow in the forest here. Some of the area is wet and boggy with grass. Other parts have heath and low plants typical of areas which have snow, and boronia, a native plant with dull flowers but beautiful perfume grows there. There are many steep mountains rising sharply from the land with waterfalls and deep valleys below, as well as the many glacial lakes. There is a lot of snow in winter and at the northern end of the walk is Cradle Mountain. This has its name because of its shape. It looks like a cradle with a man sleeping with his hands folded on his chest.
In general, Tasmania is very popular for holidays as it is always green, has good snow in winter, and is cooler than the mainland in summer. There are almost half a million people living there, only 3% of the total population. Historically it is known to Australians as having had several very strict and terrible convict settlements, for example, in the south-east at Port Arthur.

see also Australia – Areas and Regions; Convicts; Economic History; National Parks; Zeehan

Todd River

The Todd River flows, when there is water in it, through Alice Springs in Central Australia. It was named after the Postmaster General of South Australia in the early 1870s when the Overland Telegraph was built. The river starts in the MacDonnel Ranges which run east-west of Alice Springs for about 200 kilometres. The rainfall is low and very different each year and the area is a desert. Near where the river starts it has cut deep gorges through the Mac Donnells which are spectacular and beautiful, such as Simpson's Gap, Emily Gap and Trephina Gorge. These gorges very often have water even in very dry times and so have more desert plants and many birds and animals can be seen here. The river runs for about 300 kilometres, finishing in the Simpson Desert in the south east corner of the Northern Territory. Todd River is well-known for the annual boat race called the "Henley-on-Todd Regatta", **run** – literally – in August or September. Each crew competing has a boat without the bottom. The crew climbs into the boat, lifts it up and runs across the sandy river bed, as this is nearly always dry, to the finishing line. It is the only known boat race in the world to be run without water.

see also Australia – Areas and Regions;
Northern Territory

Two-Up

"Two-up" is an Australian gambling game which can only be played legally in casinos. It is played with two coins – originally pennies – which had the Queen's head on one side called "heads" and a kangaroo on the "tails" side. A small wooden board called a kip is held by the spinner, who is the person who is going to throw the coins. The spinner places the two pennies on the kip, moves his wrist and spins the pennies up into the air. The aim is that the coins fall with both heads up, then the spinner wins. A no-throw is when a head and a tail fall and with two tails the spinner loses and pays the players. Players make a circle and put their bets in front of them. If the spinner wins, he collects the money, if not he has to pay each player the amount he bet. There are many extra variations for betting such as how many heads or tails will be thrown one after another. The game was particularly popular among soldiers and was played by them during the World Wars and immediately after. Today it is not played very much as there are other legal forms of gambling.

Uluru and the Red Centre

"Uluru" is the Koori name for the world's largest monolith. Uluru, also known as "Ayer's Rock", is found in Central Australia which was an inland sea during geological history. This hard, red-brown rock rises 348 metres up out of the surrounding flat plain of red sand. Depending on the time of day and how many clouds there are, the Rock's colour varies from a deep brown to a purple-red to a deep orange. The walking track around it is about nine kilometres long and passes through light scrub – small bushes of one to two metres, high grass full of wildflowers in season and open sandy areas with some low, fine silver grass. The deep red-brown rock always rises steeply to one side, sometimes as a flat wall but often having caves or steep gullies made by the wind and rain over thousands of years. There are several waterholes, some springs and if it has rained recently, waterfalls.
Apart from Uluru, there are several 'mountains' in "The Centre". All of these rise out of flat sandy desert and are therefore impressive and can be seen for long distances.
Mount Conner, Chamber's Pillar and the Olgas are some examples. The Olgas are a small group of rounded hills grouped together just north of Ayer's Rock with a walk through the Valley of the Winds which passes through their centre. As well as hills there are also gorges and canyons which have been cut into the landscape by the wind and rain. King's Canyon has long narrow sections with water-holes and thick scrub, an area called "The Garden of Eden" and wide grassy sections with walls of brown-red cliffs around them. One very unusual area is between Alice Springs and "The Rock". It is called "Palm Valley".
In the middle of the desert is a small area along a river bed that has permanent waterholes. Ancient palms found nowhere else in the world grow here. They are directly related to the plants that grew when The Centre had a much wetter climate. Many of these areas have religious significance for the Kooris.
After a longer period without rain everything is covered with fine red-brown dust. It is very unusual to see the grey and yellow greens of the trees and other plants freshly washed and Uluru turned to a deep purple-black in the rain with water running off it. Within a few days of rain the whole area is covered with brightly

coloured wildflowers, some of which last for months as they are the everlasting flowers. The plants have adapted to the desert conditions so that they use the little rain that falls effectively. Because of this, the time plants need to grow and flower is very short.

Near The Rock, just over 400 kilometres by air, is Alice Springs. Early on there was a settlement because of the springs, as a water supply in the desert is necessary. "The Alice" was at this time a supply town for the few people who lived in the desert and also a station on the original Overland Telegraph Line connecting Australia directly with the outside world. There is also a railway running from Adelaide to Alice Springs. Today, The Alice lives very much from tourism. It is in the Mac Donnell Ranges, a low line of red-brown rock breaking the landscape from east to west. There are over ten springs and waterholes making the range the home of many birds animals and plants. It is easy to identify many different birds sitting quietly at a waterhole. Animals such as kangaroos, wallabies and emus are most often seen at dawn or dusk when they drink.

see also Australia – Areas and Regions; Kooris; National Parks; Northern Territory

Victoria

Victoria is the second smallest state in Australia. Its area of just under 2.5 thousand square kilometres makes up only about 3% of the country. Although small, the milder climate is good for farming and makes it a pleasant place to live. This can be seen by the population figure of over 4.5 million for the state. This is more than 25% of Australia's total population.
Melbourne is Victoria's capital city and during the 19th century was unofficially seen as the capital city of Australia. One of the reasons for this was that a lot of gold was found in Victoria and that brought money to the state. Later on Sydney, the capital of New South Wales, developed, and competition between the two cities for the unofficial title is still strong.
Melbourne lies on Port Phillip Bay and has many sandy beaches. The Yarra River flows through it and several rowing clubs train regularly on it. Parks are on each side of the river where it runs through the city and many office people walk along the bank during lunch-time, have a barbecue there, or go for a jog to keep fit. Melbourne people are used to the Yarra's brown colour that comes from the earth mixed into the waters in the hills where it runs quickly.
The Great Dividing Range, the mountain chain going from north to south along the east coast of Australia, finishes in Victoria. Starting with the suburbs in the south of Melbourne, the hills are large. Driving out of the city in a north-easterly direction the hills increase and the Dandenong Hills start. These have many areas of natural temperature rain-forest with tall, beautiful eucalypts. The shape of the tree tops are rounded and very different from European trees. Below these are smaller trees such as wattles or acacias with their yellow flowers or in the wetter areas tree ferns that grow up to two metres in height. Lyre birds and many other colourful birds live there.
The hills become higher and more rugged to the north of the state, and are very popular for bushwalking. Many people take a tent, sleeping-bag and food and hike for a short weekend trip or a longer holiday. It is possible to walk through forest and hills north east along the Great Dividing Range for a month, going into New South Wales and to the start of the Murray or Indigo River. Where the river is wide and deep it is the border between most of New South Wales and Victoria.
Following the Murray River west along the border of the two states the country changes. Boats used to come up this from South Australia and

were important for trade and as transport for people. Sometimes there were huge floods and the boats sailed off the river without knowing. When the floods went down overnight, the boats were left caught on the land in the middle of trees a long way from the river. One was left several kilometres away from the river and it was not possible to transport it back. The climate in this western area of Victoria is much drier and hotter than south of the Divide. The land is also much flatter. There are large irrigation schemes around the Murray River which take water long distances to improve farming. The area is well known for its citrus fruits such as oranges and grapes used for eating fresh, drying as sultanas, raisins and currants and for wine.

The central and western areas of the state are flat and dry. The further west, the drier the climate. There are several national parks there, such as "The Little Desert". This is a semi-desert area with a lot of wildlife, especially emus and kangaroos. The Wimmera River runs through it and it is easy to see twenty different birds in an afternoon while enjoying swimming. The Grampians are just west of Melbourne. These are low but rugged hills rising suddenly out of a flat plain. They are the result of volcanoes from millions of years ago. In spring they are especially beautiful with many colourful wildflowers and large mobs or groups of kangaroos and emus feed on the narrow plains between the Grampian Ranges.

The coastal area of Victoria also offers a lot of variety. Large beaches, some calm and some with surf are found all along the coast. There are also some rugged landforms such as the "Twelve Apostles" west of Melbourne. These are twelve very small, high islands with cliff sides standing in the ocean not far from the water's edge. They look like twelve men.

see also Australia – Areas and Regions; Australian Capital Territory; Economic History; National Parks; Southern Cross

Voluntary Welfare

The distance and difficulties faced by the early Australians forced them to develop independence and initiative. However, neighbours willingly helped each other and a lot of work in the early days required a number of people. Clearing the land, building a house or sheds and planting and harvesting wheat and other crops are some examples. From this back-ground, the tradition of helping others grew up. Non-Australians do not usually realise how often locals get together to do things that need to be done. It could be repairs to a house, work in the garden or just to talk something over.
The telephone books of towns and cities show how people have organised themselves into groups offering help voluntarily.
Churches are particularly active here. Telephone numbers are listed of clubs for all kinds of sports and hobbies. Other services such as "Meals On Wheels" for senior citizens and groups offering support for people with problems are just a few more examples. Most of the large fire fighting service, the Country Fire Authority, is run on a voluntary basis. The bushfires each summer are normally fought by trained volunteers who often risk their lives to save others. Special activities during the summer holidays for children and teenagers include games on the beach or in a local park, all types of sport, train trips to special places and barbecues are common. There are also some week camps for bushwalking, rock climbing and canoeing which are organised by both churches and non-church groups.
There are an estimated 37,000 non-governmental welfare organisations in Australia, using volunteer help from 1.5 million people or nearly a tenth of the entire population. If these people were paid for the work, it would add about 1.5% of the country's production.

see also Bushfires

Waltzing Matilda

"Waltzing Matilda" is the name of Australia's most popular folksong. It is about a swagman or sundowner, the name given to men who used to walk through the outback in search of work. The "swag" or "matilda" was usually a grey woollen blanket that they put their clothes and other goods in. This was then rolled together, tied with a piece of thin leather and carried over the shoulder or on the back. "To waltz" was to travel through the bush with a swag and comes from the German word meaning "to dance". This has been taken into Australian English to mean moving in a relaxed way and not in a hurry. Many men moved in the outback from station to station looking for work. Jobs such as fencing, helping with the sheep or clearing land were common.
Shearers also sometimes walked from station to station around the time the sheep had to be shorn if they did not own a horse. During the depression in the 1890s many more men took up the swag as there was no work in the cities. There was an unwritten custom that a swagman would be given flour, sugar and tea from any station as payment for a small job if no larger ones needed doing or the station owners had no cash money to pay for work.
The story of "Waltzing Matilda" is based on two stories Banjo Patterson, a famous Australian bush poet, heard while in Queensland during the 1890s. The first was that there was a waterhole in the area said to be haunted by the ghost of a man who had done something wrong. Rather than being caught by the police he jumped into a billabong, a small lake near a river, and died. The second was one day when Banjo was out riding with a friend and saw a dead sheep with just one front leg cut off. His friend told him that at times when a swagman was hungry and had no food he would kill a sheep and just take and cook what he could eat and carry for the day. The meat would not stay fresh in the heat. Banjo Patterson combined these two events and made up the song "Waltzing Matilda" which is the most popular and well known Australian folksong today.

This is the Story of "Walzing Matilda" by Banjo Patterson.

A swagman was camped by a billabong, a small lake that used to be a part of a nearby river that had changed its course. He was hungry and a jumbuck, an old male sheep, came down to the waterhole to drink. The swagman killed the sheep and was just putting it into his food or tucker bag when he got caught. A squatter, a farmer who had land and was usually a rich, and three mounted police rode by. They came down to the billabong and caught him stealing the sheep. Knowing he was in trouble, he jumped into the water and died as he did not want to give up his freedom. The billabong is said to be haunted and the swagman's voice can be heard calling out to the police and squatter, "You'll never catch me alive!"

see also Outback Life

Western Australia

Western Australia is the largest state in Australia. It covers almost a third of the continent, that is over 2.5 million square kilometres. It has 12,500 kilometres of coast and stretches about 2,400 kilometres from north to south and 1,600 kilometres from east to west at its widest point. The coastal plains of Western Australia are narrow, seldom wider than 20 kilometres. However they are very important to the state as most settlement and development has taken place on them. Perth, the capital city, is situated on the Swan River in the Southwest and is one important example. At other parts of the coast there are no plains, as in the south-east. Here along the Great Australia Bight the land stops and drops away directly in cliffs of 150 metres into the Southern Ocean. These cliffs go for hundreds of kilometres without stopping, and there is no place for a ship to anchor for more than 1,500 kilometres. The Southern Ocean coming directly from the Antarctica hits the cliffs with all the force of the Antarctic winds. When there are very strong winds, large waves can build up. These can be seen when over a kilometre away from the cliffs. When they hit, they have the force of a tidal wave. Often huge pieces of cliff crash into the ocean below.

These areas with no coastal plains are part of the great plateau which covers more than ninety per cent of the state. The land is mainly flat or gently rolling. There are a few mountain ranges such as Hammersley in the north-west where iron ore is mined and the Stirling Ranges in the south. Part of the Stirling Ranges is a National Park and the area is very popular for bushwalking. The spring wild flowers there are thick and colourful.

Blackboy palms have fine, long, firm leaves falling gracefully out and down from their centre. Here at the centre a huge, long stem with a black head grows up one or two metres above the leaves. These are typical in the area. The plateau is made of very ancient rocks from over 500 million years ago. Its economic value has been discovered in more recent times as it contains many valuable minerals.

Large areas of arid country are also part of the plateau, such as the Great Sandy Desert and the Gibson Desert. Some parts are stoney desert and others are sandy. The sandy deserts have sand dunes which may move with the wind and cover everything in their path or be stable and have channels made by streams. These streams only run when it rains or water flows in from another area. This may only happen every twenty or thirty years. There are also many salt lakes. People who do not know Australia or understand her dry climate sometimes are confused by a map in the atlas. This shows many rivers and lakes, but all the inland

rivers are normally dry and hardly ever flow, and the lakes are usually dry salt pans.
As Western Australia is so large, there are different climates in different parts. In the north, the climate is sub-tropical monsoonal with summer rain, from November to March, and a dry winter. The central desert areas have an unreliable rainfall. They are all in the area which receives less than 30 cl of rain on average each year. Many receive much less. An area having 30 cl or less rain a year is called "a desert."
The south-west region has a Mediterranean climate, with cool, wet winters and warm, dry summers. This is the area where most people live, and is very popular for its beaches and spring wild flowers.
The coastal areas normally have a sea breeze blowing onto the land in the afternoon. This cools the temperature which often reaches the high 30° or low 40°. In Perth, this breeze is called the "Fremantle Doctor". Fremantle is the city south of Perth.
Western Australia is the state with the most room and is the least densely populated. It has a population of almost 1.8 million. This is just below nine per cent of Australia's total population and over eighty per cent of these people live in cities or large towns. Perth has over sixty per cent of the state's population. There are three other cities, Bunbury and Geraldton on the west coast and Kalgoorie-Boulder in the south which have above 20,000 people.

XXXX – Queensland's Beer

Sometimes an Australian from the south might be heard asking why Queensland's beer is called "Four X" or "XXXX", and giving the answer that people cannot spell very well in the north so they just wrote four crosses on the beer barrels. This is not the reason for the name, but one of Queensland's popular beers is actually called "Four X" written as "XXXX".

The hot Australian climate makes people thirsty. Beer is easier to produce than wine, and farmers who planted vineyards last century had many problems with the climate, land and plant diseases. All these factors made beer popular. A good beer to an Australian must be cold, like ice, and must have a white head of only about one centimetre. Many European visitors find this very different from the beer they are used to.

There are many kinds of beer produced in Australia. Generally, each area or state has one or two local beers, and there are also a few sold nationally. Foster's has even begun exporting beer and producing it using the Australian recipe for the Irish and English markets, and are trying to enter the German market. Because almost everybody in Australia has a car as the public transport system is not large, many companies produce light beers which are very popular.

Visitors to an Australian pub will often hear people saying, "It's my shout." This does not mean that they will start shouting aloud, but that they are buying all their friends a drink.

see also Pubs; Queensland

Yachting (Aus & NZ)

Many people in both countries sail in their free time, is their own yacht or a hired or borrowed one. As most people live relatively near the coasts and they are so long, there are many chances to sail and many places where it is possible to sail alone. In Australia there were already yacht races in 1827, both on the Derwent River in Tasmania and on Sydney Harbour. Today there are several world famous yacht races in Australia. In the Sydney to Hobart Yacht Race, the boats leave Sydney on Boxing Day, and sail south down the east coast, across Bass Strait which separates the mainland from Tasmania, to Hobart on the east coast of Tasmania. Sydney Harbour is always crowded with thousands of small boats and yachts on this day as they wave good bye to those competing. Weather conditions make the Bass Strait area between Victoria and Tasmania and the ocean around Tasmania very dangerous and difficult to sail in. Every second year this race is part of the final event in the Southern Cross Cup.

Internationally, Australian and New Zealand yachtsmen have been successful. The Admiral's Cup races held off the English coast has been won several times by Australia, and Australia was the first country to win the America's Cup from the Americans. This was in 1983 after the Americans had held it for 132 years. They lost it in the next race to the Americans, but then New Zealand was it in 1995. Money to pay for the NZ boat was raised by selling pairs of red socks!

see also Beaches

Zeehan

Zeehan is a mining town in the western part of Tasmania, and almost 2,000 people are living there.
The west coast mountain ranges of Tasmania are very rugged and steep and covered with a thick forest.
The rainfall is almost two and a half metres each year. Several kilometres south of the town is Mount Zeehan. Abel Tasman named the mountain in 1642 after one of his ships as he sailed by on one of his voyages of discovery. Mining began in the 1880s when silver was discovered. It was mined extensively for over thirty years and the town grew rapidly.
In the early 1900s it had a population of over 8,000 and had twenty-six hotels. The town developed around the needs of the mines and the miners. During the boom it was a very rich town because there was a lot of silver. There are still some old buildings and a museum about the mines, showing how silver was mined at depths in the earth at that time. The town is a small one today, living mainly from some mining and tourists visiting the beautiful west coast. Recently, new mining extending an old mine has begun. The success of this in the future is, however, not clear.

see also Australia – Areas and Regions; Economic History; Tasmania

Vocabulary

A

acacia [ə'keɪʃə]	Akazie
Achernar ['eɪkənɑː]	Alpha (Stern)
acid ['æsɪd]	sauer
addicted [ə'dɪktɪd]	süchtig
to admonish [əd'mɒnɪʃ]	ermahnen
advanced [əd'vɑːnst]	weiterentwickelt
airfield ['eəfiːld]	Flugplatz
alga, pl. algae ['ælgə, 'ældʒiː]	Alge
alkaline ['ælkəlaɪn]	alkalihaltig
allegiance [ə'liːdʒəns]	Treue
ancestral spirits [æn'sestrəl 'spɪrɪts]	Geister der Vorfahren
to anchor ['æŋkə]	vor Anker gehen
ancient ['eɪnʃənt]	alt
angle, right angle [raɪt 'æŋgl]	Winkel, rechter Winkel
annual ['ænjʊəl]	jährlich
anti-clockwise [æntɪ'klɒkwaɪz]	gegen den Uhrzeigersinn
apex, pl. -es, apices ['eɪpeks, 'eɪpɪsiːz]	Spitze, n
approximately [ə'prɒksɪmətlɪ]	ungefähr, circa
arid ['ærɪd]	dürr, trocken
arms [ɑːmz]	Waffen
arrival [ə'raɪvl]	Ankömmling
artesian (basin, water) [ɑː'tiːzɪən beɪsn]	artesisches (Becken, Wasser)
ash [æʃ]	Asche
to assist [ə'sɪst]	unterstützen
axis, pl. axes ['æksɪs, 'æksiːz]	Achse, n

B

backwater ['bækwɔːtə]	gestautes, totes Wasser
backyard [bæk'jɑːd]	Garten hinter dem Haus
to balance ['bæləns]	im Gleichgewicht halten, ins Gleichgewicht bringen
bank [bæŋk]	Ufer
barley ['bɑːlɪ]	Gerste
bark [bɑːk]	Rinde
basin ['beɪsn]	Becken
bay [beɪ]	Bucht, Erker
beak [biːk]	Schnabel
beech [biːtʃ]	Buche
beehive ['biːhaɪv]	Bienenkorb
bet [bet]	Wetteinsatz
bill [bɪl]	Schnabel
billabong ['bɪləbɒŋ]	*Aus:* Seitenarm eines Flusses
to bind-bound-bound [baɪnd, baʊnd]	binden
birdlife ['bɜːdlaɪf]	wildlebende Vögel
blanket ['blæŋkɪt]	Decke
blunt [blʌnt]	stumpf
boarding school ['bɔːdɪŋ skuːl]	Internat
boggy ['bɒgɪ]	sumpfig
to boil [bɔɪl]	kochen
to bring to boil	zum Kochen bringen
border ['bɔːdə]	Grenze
bore [bɔː]	Bohrloch
bottletree ['bɒtltriː]	Australischer Flaschenholzbaum
breed [briːd]	Brut
breeding ['briːdɪŋ]	Fortpflanzung und Aufzucht der Jungen
breeze [briːz]	Brise
brick [brɪk]	Ziegelstein, Backstein
to bubble ['bʌbl]	sprudeln
bud [bʌd]	Knospe
budgerigar ['bʌdʒərɪgɑː]	Wellensittich
bunch [bʌntʃ]	Bündel, Büschel

burrow ['bʌrəʊ]	Bau
to burst into flames [bɜːst]	in Flammen aufgehen
to bury ['berɪ] beerdigen	begraben,
bushman ['bʊʃmən]	jemand, der im Busch lebt und arbeitet
bushranger ['bʊʃreɪndʒə]	*Aus.* Bandit

C

canoe [kə'nuː]	Kanu
capital ['kæpɪtl]	Groß-
capped [kæpt]	bedeckt
snow-capped ['snəʊkæpt]	schneebedeckt
carnival ['kɑːnɪvl]	Volksfest
cash money ['kæʃ mʌnɪ]	Bargeld
casual dress ['kæʒʊəl dres]	Freizeit-kleidung
cattle ['kætl]	Vieh
cattleman ['kætlmən]	Viehtreiber
cause [kɔːz]	Sache
cave [keɪv]	Höhle
cay [keɪ]	kleine Insel
census ['sensəs]	Volkszählung
cereal ['sɪərɪəl]	Frühstückskost aus Getreide
chain [tʃeɪn]	Kette
chained [tʃeɪnd]	eingekettet
charcoal ['tʃɑːkəʊl]	Holzkohle
charge [tʃɑːdʒ]	Anklage
cheek [tʃiːk]	Backe
chess [tʃes]	Schach
chest [tʃest]	Brust
chief [tʃiːf]	Häuptling
to chip [tʃɪp]	anschlagen, beschädigen
chop [tʃɒp]	Kotelett
chopper ['tʃɒpə]	*Aus:* Hub-schrauber
circular ['sɜːkjʊlə]	kreisförmig
claw [klɔː]	Kralle, Klaue
to clear (sth of sth) [klɪə]	(etwas von etwas) räumen
to clothe [kləʊð]	kleiden
clothes line ['kləʊðzlaɪn]	Wäscheleine
coarse [kɔːs]	grob
coastal ['kəʊstl]	Küsten-
competition [kɒmpə'tɪʃn]	Konkurrenz, Wettbewerb
complicated ['kɒmplɪkeɪtɪd]	kompliziert
compulsory [kəm'pʌlsərɪ]	obligatorisch
to conceal [kən'siːl]	verbergen
condition [kən'dɪʃn]	Bedingung, Voraus-setzung
conditional pardon [kən'dɪʃənl pɑːdn]	bedingte Begnadigung
to confine [kən'faɪn]	einsperren
confinement [kən'faɪnmənt]	Haft
to confuse [kən'fjuːz]	verwirren, durchein-anderbringen
constellation [kɒnstə'leɪʃn]	Konstellation am Sternen-himmel
constitution [kɒnstɪ'tjuːʃn]	Verfassung
content ['kɒntent]	Gehalt, Inhalt
continental shelf [kɒntɪ'nentl ʃelf]	Kontinental-schelf, Kontinental-sockel
convict ['kɒnvɪkt]	Sträfling
to convict [kən'vɪkt]	verurteilen
conviction [kən'vɪkʃn]	Verurteilung
cookatoo [kʊkə'tuː]	Kakadu
cool [kuːl]	kühl
to cool [kuːl]	(sich) abkühlen
coral reef [kɒrəl 'riːf]	Korallenriff
cotton ['kɒtn]	Baumwolle
counter ['kaʊntə]	Theke
cove [kəʊv]	(kleine) Bucht
cradle ['kreɪdl]	Wiege
craft [krɑːft]	Boot, Schiff
crawl [krɔːl]	Kraul (Stil)
to crawl [krɔːl]	kraulen
cream [kriːm]	cremefarben
creek [kriːk]	Bach

crimson ['krɪmzn] purpurrot; Purpur
crisp [krɪsp] knusprig
critic ['krɪtɪk] Kritiker/in
crop [krɒp] (Feld)frucht
cross-section [krɒs'sekʃn] Querschnitt
crow [krəʊ] Krähe
to crush [krʌʃ] quetschen, zerquetschen
crust [krʌst] Kruste
curved [kɜːvd] gebogen, gekrümmt
currant ['kʌrənt] Korinthe, Johannisbeere
current ['kʌrənt] gegenwärtig
cygnet ['sɪgnɪt] Schwan (poetisch); Schwanenjunges

D

dairy ['deərɪ] Molkerei, Milch-
dam [dæm] Damm, Stausee
damp [dæmp] feucht
damper ['dæmpə] *Aus:* Fladenbrot
daring ['deərɪŋ] waghalsig
delicacy ['delɪkəsɪ] Delikatesse
dense [dens] dicht
depot ['depəʊ] (Lager)haus
to descend from [dɪ'send frəm] abstammen von
desert ['dezət] Wüste
destruction [dɪ'strʌkʃn] Zerstörung
destructive [dɪ'strʌktɪv] zerstörerisch
determination [dɪtɜːmɪ'neɪʃn] Entschlossenheit
device [dɪ'vaɪs] Vorrichtung
diameter [daɪ'æmɪtə] Durchmesser
to dig [dɪg, dʌg] graben, bohren
digger ['dɪgə] Goldgräber
to digest [dɪ'dʒest] verdauen
to dip [dɪp] tauchen
direction [dɪ'rekʃn] Richtung
discovery [dɪ'skʌvərɪ] Entdeckung
distances ['dɪstənsɪz] Abstände
disease [dɪ'ziːz] Krankheit
dish [dɪʃ] Schüssel; Gericht
to dissolve [dɪ'zɒlv] sich auflösen
distant ['dɪstənt] entfernt
dough [dəʊ] Teig
drainage ['dreɪnɪdʒ] Drainage, Entwässerung
drive [draɪv] Antrieb
to drop off [drɒp 'ɒf] abfallen
droplet ['drɒplɪt] Tröpfchen
drought [draʊt] Dürre
drover ['drəʊvə] Viehtreiber
dumb [dʌm] dumm
dune [djuːn] Düne
dusk [dʌsk] (Abend)dämmerung
dust [dʌst] Staub

E

eagle ['iːgl] Adler
ecosystem ['iːkəʊsɪstəm] Ökosystem
emigrant ['emɪgrənt] Auswanderer
to enclose [ɪn'kləʊz] einschließen, umgeben
enquiry [ɪn'kwaɪərɪ] Untersuchung
epoxy resin ['epɒksɪ rezɪn] Epoxydharz
Estonia [e'stəʊnɪə] Estland
eucalyptus tree [juːkə'lɪptəs triː] Eukalyptusbaum
to evaporate [ɪ'væpəreɪt] verdunsten
everlasting flower [evə'lɑːstɪŋ flaʊə] Immortelle; Strohblume
to evolve [ɪ'vɒlv] sich entwickeln
explorer [ɪk'splɔːrə] Forscher/in, Forschungsreisende/r
extended family [ɪkstendɪd 'fæməlɪ] Großfamilie
external [ɪk'stɜːnl] äußere(r,s)

F

to fan (out) [fæn] — (sich) fächerförmig ausbreiten
feature ['fi:tʃə] — Merkmal, Kennzeichen
federation [fedə'reɪʃn] — Föderation, Staatenbund
to feed-fed-fed [fi:d, fed] — fressen
to feed on ['fi:d ɒn] — sich ernähren von
fence [fens] — Zaun
to fence in [fens 'ɪn] — einzäunen
fern [fɜ:n] — Farn
fibre ['faɪbə] — Faser
fiery ['faɪərɪ] — feurig
finishing post ['fɪnɪʃɪŋ pəʊst] — Zielpfosten
fire break ['faɪə breɪk] — Feuerschneise
firm [fɜ:m] — fest
to fit into [fɪt 'ɪntə] — sich anpassen
to fit with ['fɪt wɪð] — ausstatten mit
flagpole ['flægpəʊl] — Fahnenstange
flap [flæp] — Klappe; Lappen
to flatten ['flætn] — flach machen
flavour ['fleɪvə] — Geschmack, Aroma
fleet [fli:t] — Flotte
flight [flaɪt] — Flucht
flightless ['flaɪtlɪs] — flugunfähig
to float [fləʊt] — schweben
flock [flɒk] — Schwarm, Schar
flood [flʌd] — Hochwasser, Überschwemmung
fluffy ['flʌfɪ] — flaumig
fluid ['flu:ɪd] — flüssig
forebear [fɔ:'beə] — Ahn(e)
forefinger ['fɔ:fɪŋgə] — Zeigefinger
forested ['fɒrɪstɪd] — bewaldet
four-wheel drive [fɔ:wi:l'draɪv] — Allradantrieb
fragile ['frædʒaɪl] — empfindlich
frame [freɪm] — Rahmen
to frighten ['fraɪtn] — erschrecken
frog [frɒg] — Frosch
fur [fɜ:] — Pelz, Fell

G

to gamble ['gæmbl] — (um Geld) spielen, sich an einem Glücksspiel beteiligen
gambling game ['gæmblɪŋ geɪm] — Glücksspiel
gaol = jail [dʒeɪl] — Gefängnis
garlic ['gɑ:lɪk] — Knoblauch
genuine ['dʒenjʊɪn] — authentisch, ungekünstelt
ghost [gəʊst] — Geist, Geister-
giant ['dʒaɪənt] — riesig
gill [gɪl] — Kiemen
glacial ['gleɪsɪəl] — Gletscher-, eisig
glacier ['glæsɪə] — Gletscher
glow-worm ['gləʊwɜ:m] — Glühwürmchen
glue [glu:] — Leim
gnat [næt] — (Stech)mücke
goanna [gəʊ'ænɑ:] — Waran
goddess ['gɒdɪs] — Göttin
goldrush ['gəʊldrʌʃ] — Goldrausch
gorge [gɔ:dʒ] — Schlucht
gossip ['gɒsɪp] — Klatsch, Tratsch
graceful ['greɪsfl] — anmutig
grain [greɪn] — Korn
grape [greɪp] — Traube
gravity ['grævətɪ] — Schwerkraft
graveyard ['greɪvjɑ:d] — Friedhof
to graze [greɪz] — weiden (lassen); abweiden, abgrasen
grease-proof paper [gri:spru:f 'peɪpə] — Butterbrotpapier
grip [grɪp] — Griff
grotto ['grɒtəʊ] — Grotte, Höhle
to grunt [grʌnt] — grunzen
gulf [gʌlf] — Golf
gully ['gʌlɪ] — Schlucht
gum [gʌm] — Harz
gum = gum tree ['gʌmtri:] — Eukalyptusbaum

H

handle ['hændl]	Griff
to handle ['hændl]	umgehen mit, handhaben
harvest ['hɑːvɪst]	Ernte
to harvest ['hɑːvɪst]	ernten
to hatch [hætʃ]	ausschlüpfen
to haunt [hɔːnt]	verfolgen
heath [hiːθ]	Heide
highlight ['haɪlaɪt]	Höhepunkt
hollow ['hɒləʊ]	hohl
hothouse ['hɒthaʊs]	Treibhaus
hover ['hɒvə]	Schweben
to howl [haʊl]	heulen

I

ice age ['aɪs eɪdʒ]	Eiszeit
to identify [aɪ'dentɪfaɪ]	identifizieren
impermeable [ɪm'pɜːmɪəbl]	undurchlässig
implementation [ɪmplɪmen'teɪʃn]	Durchführung
impostor [ɪm'pɒstə]	Betrüger/in
inferno [ɪn'fɜːnəʊ]	Inferno; Flammen-meer
infiltration [ɪnfɪl'treɪʃn]	Durchsickern
inflatable [ɪn'fleɪtəbl]	aufblasbar
inhabitant [ɪn'hæbɪtənt]	Einwohner/in
to initiate [ɪ'nɪʃɪəɪt]	feierlich aufnehmen, initiieren
instance ['ɪnstəns]	Fall
iodite ['aɪədaɪt]	Jodid
to irrigate ['ɪrɪgeɪt]	bewässern
irrigation [ɪrɪ'geɪʃn]	Bewässerung
isle [aɪl]	Eiland

J

jewellery ['dʒuːəlrɪ]	Schmuck
to join together [dʒɔɪn tə'geðə]	sich vereinigen
judgement ['dʒʌdʒmənt]	Urteils-vermögen
jumbuk ['dʒʌmbʌk]	*Aus:* alter Schafbock

K

to keep alive [kiːp ə'laɪv]	am Leben bleiben
kettle ['ketl]	Kessel
kingfisher ['kɪŋfɪʃə]	Eisvogel
kite [kaɪt]	(Spielzeug) drachen
to knock out [nɒk 'aʊt]	bewußtlos schlagen, k.o. schlagen

L

lace work ['leɪswɜːk]	Filigran (muster)
lagoon [lə'guːn]	Lagune
to lamb [læm]	lammen, ein Lamm werfen
landmark ['lændmɑːk]	Naturzeichen, Meilenstein, Markstein
landscape ['lændskeɪp]	Landschaft
larva, pl. larvae ['lɑːvə, lɑːviː]	Larve, n
lash [læʃ]	Peitsche, Peitschenhieb
Latvia ['lætvɪə]	Lettland
law enforcement [lɔː ɪn'fɔːsmənt]	Gesetzes-vollzug
lemon ['lemən]	Zitrone
to lick [lɪk]	lecken
limestone ['laɪmstəʊn]	Kalkstein
liquid ['lɪkwɪd]	Flüssigkeit
literally ['lɪtərəlɪ]	buchstäblich
Lithuania [lɪθjuː'eɪnɪə]	Litauen
to live on ['lɪv ɒn]	sich ernähren von
lizard ['lɪzəd]	Eidechse
location [ləʊ'keɪʃn]	Lage, Position
to lope [ləʊp]	(in großen Sätzen) springen, hoppeln
lounge [laʊndʒ]	Salon
lyre ['laɪə]	Leier

M

mail [meɪl] Post
maintenance ['meɪntənəns] Wartung, Pflege
mammal ['mæml] Säugetier
mangrove ['mæŋgrəʊv] Mangrovenbaum
to manoeuver [mə'nu:və] manövrieren
to map [mæp] eine Landkarte anfertigen von
mark [mɑ:k] Mal
marking ['mɑ:kɪŋ] Zeichnung
marsh [mɑ:ʃ] Sumpf
marsupial [mɑ:'su:pɪəl] Beuteltier
matilda [mə'tɪldə] *Aus:* Reisebündel
mating time ['meɪtɪŋ taɪm] Paarungszeit
mature [mə'tjʊə] reif, ausgewachsen
medical ['medɪkl] medizinisch, ärztlich
Mediterranean (Sea) [medɪtə'reɪnɪən] Mittelmeer
to mend [mend] reparieren
to merge [mɜ:dʒ] ineinander übergehen
merino [mə'ri:nəʊ] Merinoschaf
messmate ['mesmeɪt] Eukalyptusbaum
migrant ['maɪgrənt] Wanderarbeiter/in, Gastarbeiter/in
to migrate [maɪ'greɪt] (ab-,aus) wandern
mild [maɪld] mild, leicht
Milky Way [mɪlkɪ 'weɪ] Milchstraße
to mine [maɪn] abbauen
mineral content ['mɪnərəl 'kɒntent] Mineralgehalt
mineral resources ['mɪnərəl rɪ'sɔ:sɪz] Bodenschätze
minister ['mɪnɪstə] Pfarrer
mirage ['mɪrɑ:ʒ] Fata Morgana, Luftspiegelung
missionary ['mɪʃənrɪ] Missionar
mob [mɒb] Herde, Schar
modern conveniences (pl.) [mɒdn kən'vi:nɪənsɪz] moderner Komfort
moist [mɔɪst] feucht
momentum [mə'mentəm] Schwung
monotreme ['mɒnətri:m] Kloakentier (Säugetiere, die Eier legen)
monsoon [mɒn'su:n] Monsun
mound [maʊnd] Hügel
mountain ash [maʊntɪn 'æʃ] Eberesche
mountain range [maʊntɪn 'reɪndʒ] Bergkette
mud pool ['mʌd pu:l] Schlammtümpel
muscle ['mʌsl] Muskel
to muster ['mʌstə] zusammentreiben

N

need [ni:d] Bedürfnis
needle ['ni:dl] Nadel
nocturnal [nɒk'tɜ:nl] Nacht-
nostril ['nɒstrəl] Nasenloch
notice ['nəʊtɪs] Notiz
noxious ['nɒkʃəs] schädlich
nursery rhyme ['nɜ:sərɪ raɪm] Kinderlied, Kinderreim
nut [nʌt] Nuß

O

occasion [ə'keɪʒn] Gelegenheit
occasionally, on some occasions [ə'keɪʒnəlɪ] gelegentlich
ochre ['əʊkə] Ocker
off the coast [ɒf ðə 'kəʊst] vor der Küste
operator ['ɒpəreɪtə] Dame/Herr von der Telefonvermittlung
orchard ['ɔ:tʃəd] Obstplantage, Obstgarten

orchid ['ɔ:kɪd]	Orchidee
organ pipe ['ɔ:gən paɪp]	Orgelpfeife
ornament [ɔ:nəmənt]	Ziergegenstand; Verzierung
ostrich ['ɒstrɪtʃ]	Strauß
ounce [aʊns]	Unze
outback, the outback ['aʊtbæk]	der (australische) Busch
outboard motor [aʊtbɔ:d 'məʊtə]	Außenbordmotor
outcrop of rock ['aʊtkrɒp əv rɒk]	Felsnase
ox, pl. oxen [ɒks, 'ɒksn]	Ochse, n

P

paddock ['pædək]	Koppel
palm [pɑ:m]	Handfläche
passage ['pæsɪdʒ]	Gang, Flur
pawpaw [pə'pɔ:]	Papaya
to pedal ['pedl]	das Pedal treten
to peel [pi:l]	schälen
pen [pen]	Pferch
perfume ['pɜ:fju:m]	Parfum
to perish ['perɪʃ]	umkommen, untergehen
pewter ['pju:tə]	Zinn
to pierce [pɪəs]	durchstoßen
pinch [pɪntʃ]	Prise
pine [paɪn]	Kiefer
pineapple ['paɪnæpl]	Ananas
pink [pɪŋk]	rosa, rosafarben
pipe [paɪp]	Rohr, Leitung
placental [plə'sentl]	Plazenta-
plague [pleɪg]	Seuche
plain [pleɪn]	Ebene, Flachland
plane [pleɪn]	Ebene
plant [plɑ:nt]	Werk
plate [pleɪt]	Platte
platypus ['plætɪpəs]	Schnabeltier
plentiful ['plentɪfl]	reichlich, im Überfluß vorhanden
ply [plaɪ]	schichtig
five-ply ['faɪvplaɪ]	fünfschichtig
plywood ['plaɪwʊd]	Sperrholz
pod [pɒd]	Hülse
point [pɔɪnt]	spitz
to point towards [pɔɪnt tə'wɔ:dz]	zeigen auf
pointed ['pɔɪntɪd]	spitz
poison ['pɔɪzn]	Gift
to poison ['pɔɪzn]	vergiften
to poke [pəʊk]	stoßen, stochern
to polish ['pɒlɪʃ]	polieren
pool [pu:l]	Teich, Loch
poor [pɔ:]	schlecht
to populate ['pɒpjʊleɪt]	besiedeln, bevölkern
porous ['pɔ:rəs]	porös
possession [pə'zeʃn]	Besitz
possum ['pɒsəm]	Possum, Beutelratte
post [pəʊst]	Pfosten
postage stamp ['pəʊstɪdʒ stæmp]	Briefmarke
postmaster general [pəʊstmɑ:stə 'dʒenrəl]	Postminister
post-war [pəʊst'wɔ:]	Nachkriegs-
pouch [paʊtʃ]	Beutel
poverty ['pɒvətɪ]	Armut
prayer [preə]	Gebet
preacher ['pri:tʃə]	Prediger
precious ['preʃəs]	wertvoll
precision [prɪ'sɪʒn]	Genauigkeit, Präzision
preferential voting [prefə'renʃl vəʊtɪŋ]	Präferenzwahlsystem
present ['preznt]	Gegenwart, Geschenk
to preserve [prɪ'zɜ:v]	schützen, erhalten
prevention of bushfire [prɪ'venʃn əv 'bʊʃfaɪə]	Feuerschutz
priest [pri:st]	Priester
private ['praɪvɪt]	Gefreiter
probability [prɒbə'bɪlətɪ]	Wahrscheinlichkeit
procedure [prə'si:dʒə]	Verfahren
to proceed from [prə'si:d frəm]	kommen von
proper ['prɒpə]	richtig
to prove oneself [pru:v]	sich erweisen als

provided [prə'vaɪdɪd]	vorausgesetzt, daß
pulpit ['pʊlpɪt]	Kanzel
pure-bred ['pjʊəbred]	reinrassig
purple ['pɜːpl]	lila, lilafarben

R

rabbit ['ræbɪt]	Kaninchen
to raft [rɑːft]	auf einem Floß fahren
rainbow ['reɪnbəʊ]	Regenbogen
rainfall ['reɪnfɔːl]	Niederschlag
rainforest ['reɪnfɒrɪst]	Regenwald
ram [ræm]	Widder, Schafbock
raspberry ['rɑːzbrɪ]	Himbeere
rate [reɪt]	Tempo
ray [reɪ]	Strahl
recovery [rɪ'kʌvərɪ]	Erholung
recreation facilities [rekrɪ'eɪʃn fə'sɪlətɪ]	Möglichkeiten zur Freizeitgestaltung
red currant [red 'kʌrənt]	rote Johannisbeere
redwood ['redwʊd]	roter Sandholzbaum
reef [riːf]	Riff
to reflect [rɪ'flekt]	spiegeln, widerspiegeln
to reflect off [rɪ'flekt ɒf]	zurückwerfen, reflektieren
reflection [rɪ'flekʃn]	Spiegelung, Widerspiegelung, Spiegelbild
refrigeration [rɪfrɪdʒə'reɪʃn]	Kühlung, Tiefkühlung
to refrigerate [rɪ'frɪdʒəreɪt]	kühlen, tiefkühlen
refugee [refjʊ'dʒiː]	Flüchtling
to be reincarnated [riː'ɪnkɑːneɪtɪd]	wiedergeboren werden
to rely on [rɪ'laɪ ɒn]	sich auf jdn/etw verlassen
representative [reprɪ'zentətɪv]	Abgeordnete/r
resin ['rezɪn]	Harz
resuscitation [rɪsʌsɪ'teɪʃn]	Wiederbelebung
ridge [rɪdʒ]	Kamm, Grat
ring [rɪŋ]	Manege
roar [rɔː]	Gebrüll
Roman ['rəʊmən]	römisch
root [ruːt]	Wurzel
to rot [rɒt]	faulen, verfaulen
to round up [raʊnd 'ʌp]	zusammentreiben
rounded ['raʊndɪd]	abgerundet
roustabout ['raʊstəbaʊt]	*Aus:* Helfer beim Scheren
rubber duckie ['rʌbədʌkɪ]	Rettungsschlauchboot
rugged ['rʌgɪd]	felsig, zerklüftet
ruggedness ['rʌgɪdnɪs]	Zerklüftetheit
rump [rʌmp]	Hinterteil
to run [rʌn]	führen, leiten, betreiben
runoff ['rʌnɒf]	Abfluß, oberflächlich abfließendes Wasser

S

sacred ['seɪkrɪd]	heilig
salmon ['sæmən]	Lachs
to sand down [sænd 'daʊn]	abschmirgeln
savoury ['seɪvərɪ]	pikant
scale [skeɪl]	Schuppen; Maßstab
scoop [skuːp]	Kugel
to be in a scrape [skreɪp]	*Aus:* in der Klemme sitzen
scrub [skrʌb]	Gestrüpp, Busch(land)
sea-level ['siːlevl]	Meeresspiegel
sealed road [siːld]	geteerte Straße
sealer ['siːlə]	Robbenfänger
seaman ['siːmən]	Seemann
to secrete [sɪ'kriːt]	verbergen
seed [siːd]	Samen

to seed [siːd]	zur Saat bringen, kommen
to seep [siːp]	sickern
seldom ['seldəm]	selten
semi- ['semɪ]	Halb-
to sense [sens]	fühlen, spüren
sensitive ['sensətɪv]	sensibel, empfindlich
servant ['sɜːvənt]	Diener/in
settlement ['setlmənt]	Siedlung
shade [ʃeɪd]	Schatten; (Farb)ton
shallow ['ʃæləʊ]	flach, seicht
shark [ʃɑːk]	Hai
sharp [ʃɑːp]	scharf, spitz
to shear-shore-shorn [ʃɪə, ʃɔː, ʃɔːn]	scheren
shearer ['ʃɪərə]	Scherer
shed [ʃed]	Schuppen
sheltered ['ʃeltəd]	geschützt
shrimp [ʃrɪmp]	Krabbe(n)
shrub [ʃrʌb]	Busch,Strauch
Silesia [saɪ'liːzɪə]	Schlesien
silver ['sɪlvə]	Silber; silberfarben
single ['sɪ ŋgl]	ledig
slender ['slendə]	Schrank
smoothly ['smuːðlɪ]	ruhig, gleichmäßig
snake [sneɪk]	Schlange
to snap at ['snæp ət]	schnappen nach
sociable ['səʊʃəbl]	gesellig
social ['səʊʃl]	gesell-schaftlich
soil [sɔɪl]	Boden
soprano [sə'prɑːnəʊ]	Sopran
sorter ['sɔːtə]	Sortierer/in
space [speɪs]	Raum-, Weltraum, Platz
spear [spɪə]	Speer
spin [spɪn]	Dreh, Drehung
to spin-spun-spun [spɪn, spʌn]	sich drehen, (hoch-)werfen
spike [spaɪk]	Stachel
splash [splæʃ]	Spritzer
to splash	spritzen
spread [spred]	(Brot)aufstrich
spring [sprɪŋ]	Quelle

to squat [skwɒt]	sich (illegal) ansiedeln
stamen ['steɪmən]	Staubgefäß
state [steɪt]	Zustand
station, cattle/ sheep station ['steɪʃn]	*Aus:* Farm, Vieh-/Schaf-zuchtfarm
to steepen ['stiːpən]	steiler machen
stem [stem]	Stiel
sticky ['stɪkɪ]	klebrig
stiff [stɪf]	steif
sting [stɪŋ]	Stich
stingray ['stɪŋreɪ]	Stachelrochen
stockade [stɒ'keɪd]	Palisaden (-zaun/-wand)
stock exchange ['stɒk ɪsktʃeɪndʒ]	Börse
stockman ['stɒkmən]	Viehzüchter; Farmarbeiter
stone age ['stəʊn eɪdʒ]	Steinzeit
storage ['stɔːrɪdʒ]	Speicherung, Speicher, Lager
storey ['stɔːrɪ]	Stockwerk
strait [streɪt]	Meerenge, Straße
stranded ['strændɪd]	gestrandet
stream [striːm]	Strom
string [strɪŋ]	Faden, Schnur, Saite
strip [strɪp]	Streifen
sufficient [sə'fɪʃnt]	genügend
suffrage ['sʌfrɪdʒ]	Wahlrecht
sugar cane ['ʃʊgə keɪn]	Zuckerrohr
sulphur ['sʌlfə]	Schwefel
sultana [sʌl'tɑːnə]	Sultanine
sundowner ['sʌndaʊnə]	*Aus:* Vaga-bunden, Landstreicher
surf [sɜːf]	Brandung
swag [swæg]	*Aus:* Reise-bündel
swagman ['swægmən]	*Aus:* Land-streicher
swamp [swɒmp]	Sumpf
swan [swɒn]	Schwan
sweep = sweepstake [swiːp, 'swiːpsteɪk]	*beim Pferderennen: jede/r zieht den Namen eines Pferdes und zahlt ein, der Gewinn wird geteilt*

to swing [swɪŋ, swʌŋ] schwingen, sich schwingen
to swirl [swɜːl] wirbeln
synthetic fibre [sɪn'θetɪk faɪbə] Kunstfaser

T

tail [teɪl] Schwanz; Zahl (Seite einer Münze)
to take flight [teɪk 'flaɪt] die Flucht ergreifen
to take up [teɪk 'ʌp] greifen zu, zur Hand nehmen
taper ['teɪpə] Spitze
taste [teɪst] Geschmack
to tattoo [tə'tuː] tätowieren
temperate ['tempərət] gemäßigt
term [tɜːm] Semester, Trimester, Quartal, Ausdruck
terrace house ['terəs haʊs] Reihenhaus
territorial [terə'tɔːrɪəl] Revier-
territory ['terətrɪ] Territorium
thorn [θɔːn] Dorn
thumb [θʌm] Daumen
thunder ['θʌndə] Donner
to thunder ['θʌndə] brüllen
to tie [taɪ] binden
to tighten ['taɪtn] fester machen, anziehen
tile [taɪl] (Dach)ziegel
timber ['tɪmbə] Holz
tinfoil [tɪn'fɔɪl] Aluminiumfolie
tiny ['taɪnɪ] winzig
toe [təʊ] Zehe
to tone [təʊn] (im Farbton) harmonieren
top hat [tɒp 'hæt] Zylinder
to trade for ['treɪd fə] tauschen gegen
trade barriers ['treɪd bærɪəz] Handelsschranken
transportation [trænspɔː'teɪʃn] Deportation
trap [træp] Falle
to trap [træp] einfangen, gefangen nehmen
tray [treɪ] (Back)blech
trial ['traɪəl] Gerichtsverfahren
Tropic of Capricorn ['trɒpɪk əf 'kæprɪkɔːn] Wendekreis des Steinbocks
tropical ['trɒpɪkl] tropisch
tropics ['trɒpɪks] Tropen
trough [trɒf] Trog
trunk [trʌŋk] Stamm
to try [traɪ] vor Gericht stellen
tub [tʌb] (Bade)wanne
tucker bag ['tʌkəbæg] *Aus:* Proviantbeutel
turning point ['tɜːnɪŋ pɔɪnt] Wendepunkt
twist [twɪst] Zopf (Backwaren)
twist, a twist of the wrist [twɪst, rɪst] eine schnelle Bewegung des Handgelenkes
to twist (round) [twɪst 'raʊnd] wickeln (um)
twisted ['twɪstɪd] gedreht, verbogen
two-way radio [tuːweɪ 'reɪdɪəʊ] Funksprechgerät

U

undergrowth ['ʌndəgrəʊθ] Gestrüpp, Unterholz
to unlock [ʌn'lɒk] erschließen
unreliable [ʌnrɪ'laɪəbl] unzuverlässig
unsealed road [ʌn'siːld] nicht asphaltierte (Land) Straße
upstream [ʌp'striːm] stromaufwärts

V

valley ['vælɪ]	Tal
vegetarian [vedʒɪ'teərɪən]	Pflanzenfresser, Vegetarier
Victorian [vɪk'tɔːrɪən]	viktorianisch (aus der Zeit Königin Viktorias von England, 1837-1901)
vine [vaɪn]	Rebe
vinegar ['vɪnɪgə]	Essig
vineyard ['vɪnjəd]	Weinberg
volcanic [vɒl'kænɪk]	Vulkan-
volunteer [vɒlən'tɪə]	Freiwillige/r

W

to waltz [wɔːls]	Walzer tanzen
watch [wɒtʃ]	Wache
water-resistant ['wɔ,tərɪzɪstənt]	wasserbeständig
wattle ['wɒtl]	australische Akazie
wax [wæks]	Wachs
weapon ['wepən]	Waffe
web [web]	Spinnwebe
webbed foot [webd 'fʊt]	Schwimmfuß
whaler ['weɪlə]	Walfänger
wheat [wiːt]	Weizen
whipped cream ['wɪpt kriːm]	Schlagsahne
winding ['waɪndɪŋ]	kurvenreich
winning post ['wɪnɪŋ pəʊst]	Zielpfosten
wire ['waɪə]	Draht
wise [waɪz]	weise
womb [wuːm]	Gebärmutter
woolshed ['wʊlʃed]	Wollschuppen
worm [wɜːm]	Wurm
to worship ['wɜːʃɪp]	anbeten

Y

to yacht [jɒt]	(sport)segeln
yeast [jiːst]	Hefe
yolk, egg yolk ['eg jəʊk]	Eigelb

Teachers' Notes

General Suggestions for Teaching

Grammatical Structures
- questions, open and closed
- answering questions accurately
- contrast and comparison
- descriptions
- adjectives and adverbs

Methods

– **individual work,**
especially for the activation of passive vocabulary and further expansion of this and the formulation of questions, for example:

before a section is read or when the title has been briefly explained; *activity*: the learner notes down key or picture words (verbs, nouns, adjectives and adverbs) at random, as a list, as in brainstorming or in the form of a mindmap if the concept has been introduced; *content:* picture words that could be associated with the title of an entry;

after the entry has been read or during/after the discussion; *activity:* to write down questions; *content:* questions about words or phrases not understood, points where more information from the group or another source could be interesting or useful;

as a follow-up exercise after the lesson; *activity:* use of picture words to form the basis of a summary or a short essay; *content:* a summary of the entry or a topic related to the entry such as comparisons and contrasts between the article and the situation in the learner's area, country or continent, or a topic for creative thinking

– **pair or small group work,**
especially for the oral activation of vocabulary, the use of questions and answering these accurately, for example:

at the beginning of the lesson when the title of the entry has been written for the class to see; *activity:* asking and answering questions to illicit information and check information and understanding; *content:* using the title as a basis for the learners to gather as much information about the topic and possible comparisons and contrasts to their own country, and questions that could be clarified;
Note: In a group of more than two, the following roles are possible: one asking the question; one answering the question or passing it on to someone else for help; one observer to check the correct grammatical form of the questions and answers and ensure an immediate repetition if either is not correct and; a note taker responsible for: (i) noting down the picture words or questions for the whole class and (ii) speaking for the group if a report is made. The roles could be changed during the activity or rotated with each new group activity.

Activities

introduction to the book
- on a piece of paper each student sketches a rough map of: (i) Australia, a square if the real shape is unknown and (ii) New Zealand. On these any cities or places of interest (natural features, locations of friends or relatives . . .) are marked;
- in pairs or small groups the maps are compared and discussed, emphasis on asking and answering questions correctly;

– large outlines of Australia and New Zealand are placed on the board and members from each group take turns at explaining to the class the location (north/south/east/west or above /below/left/right) of one or two points; the actual location should be discussed and then checked finally with an atlas;
– the latitude including the Tropic of Capricorn marking the division between the tropical and sub-tropical areas, the location of both countries with respect to the whole globe should be discussed in groups, as a class or handed out depending on time;
– students should draw another rough map of both countries or receive a handout and a comparison to the size of Europe should be made by students writing around the coast of each the European country they think would be touched if the maps were placed on a map of Europe; group and/or class discussion work or direct reference to **Australia – Areas and Regions** and **New Zealand – Areas and Regions** follows;

Ideas for specific entries

Below are suggestions in point form of topics for discussion or follow-up work at home for some of the entries. Pair or small group work, possibly preceded by individual, allows speaking practice and develops the skill of finding key words.

Beaches – free time activities and the factors which influence this; explanation for differences in different areas (e.g. climate and space)

Bushfires – the most terrible personal experience had outside in the city or country; the most dangerous natural disaster for the local area or country

Convicts – punishment of criminals – ideas for change of the current system

Farming and **Cattlemen in Choppers** – modern farming in different areas today; the advantages and disadvantages of a closed market such as the EC

Immigration and **The Irish** – the population structure of the country where students come from

Kooris, The Dreamtime and **The Maoris** – comparisons and contrasts amongst: (i) other groups of people who inhabited areas before the West Europeans entered these; (ii) Western Europe today and the modern society; totems of modern western society, e.g. sports clubs, peer groups and other social and political groups in society

Rabbits – 'friend or foe' – other birds, animals or plants have their place in the environment in one area but are a problem in another

Rain-Making – the value of water – the amount of water used by one person each day

School of the Air – the advantages and disadvantages of this way of learning; suggestions of other alternatives

Voluntary Welfare – the number and type of such organisations that exist in reader's country; the advantages and disadvantages for the individual and the community

Waltzing Matilda – songs from Australia or New Zealand, either old or modern for discussion of the content and development of music

Fotonachweise

Archiv für Kunst und Geschichte, Berlin: S. 32, 40

Australia Post S. 21, 22, 23, 26, 27, 32, 33, 34, 38, 54, 57, 58, 59, 81, 85, 93

BAVARIA, Düsseldorf: S. 18/Lange, 55/Stock Imagery

Bush Fire Council of N.S.W, Australia: S. 92

Robyn Christensen: S. 17, 19, 24, 31, 41, 45, 46, 47, 49, 58, 61, 64, 71, 75, 83

Foto dpa, Frankfurt/M: U1.2, 12, 78, 84

IFA-Bilderteam, Düsseldorf: S. 7, 30, 37, 40, 41, 53, 63, 66, 77, 78, 82, 86, 96, 98

Keystone Pressedienst, Hamburg: S. 10, 12, 16, 20, 37, 43, 48, 50, 56, 60, 66, 67, 69, 77, 85, 90, 95, 97

Helga Lade Fotoagentur GmbH, Berlin: S. 6, 7, 9, 13, 14, 15, 16, 24, 25, 26, 28, 29, 35, 36, 39, 44, 48, 51, 54, 61, 62, 63, 68, 70, 76, 77, 79, 80, 87, 88, 89, 91, 94

New Zealand Tourist Board, Frankfurt: S. U 3, 37, 42, 65, 67

Pacific Way Dec 1991/Jan 1992, Air New Zealand: S. 72

Reader's Digest 6/91: S. 21

Marion Schweitzer Fotoagentur, München: S. U1, 84